Great Big Beautiful Doll

Great Big Beautiful Doll

THE ANNA NICOLE SMITH STORY

Eric and D'eva Redding

BARRICADE BOOKS / NEW YORK

Published by Barricade Books Inc.
150 Fifth Avenue
New York, NY 10011

Printed in the United States of America.

Library of Congress Cataloging-in-Publication Data

Redding, D'eva.
The Anna Nicole Smith story / by D'eva and Eric Redding.
p. cm.
ISBN 1-56980-079-0
1. Smith, Anna Nicole.   2. Celebrities—Bioghraphy.   3.Texas—Biography.
I. Redding, Eric. II. Title.
CT275.S52415 1996
973.92'092—dc20
[B]   95-50720
                                                             CIP

First Printing

Dedication

*I*n today's fast-paced society, that is filled with divorce and family squabbles and constant disharmony among our races, it is only fitting that D'eva and I dedicate this book to one another for being able to endure and nurture each other during our eight years of marriage.

Besides the normal ups and downs of any relationship...our destiny together is evident in the fact that through it all...and especially through the peaks and valleys of working together on this book...we still love one another and love our chosen time here on Earth together as husband and wife, friend and foe, and lovers of life!

This book would not have been at all possible either for the undeniable fact that we had unselfish and unequivocal support from our literary agent Charlotte Dial Breeze...we thank you one million times over!!

And of course, bless you Jolie Kramer for helping make the Anna Nicole Smith Story come to life...thank you, thank you, thank you!!! Many thanks for just being our friend.

Last of all, and certainly most important, this book would not have been possible at all if God had not given us Anna Nicole Smith to write about. We are eternally grateful to you for coming into our life and most assuredly changing our lives for some time to gome. See ya...

Foreword

D'eva and I turned on the television one night and found ourselves watching a horror show. It wasn't Freddy Krueger or a hockey-masked Jason—we wished it had been. No, what we saw was much more real and certainly more scary. We saw a friend self-destruct.

A once-stunning girl, still young at twenty-eight, was a caricature of the beauty she had been. Her moment in the spotlight continues, but now its harsh glare illuminates dissipation instead of happiness.

It was a rerun of *The Howard Stern Show*. D'eva and I are not fans of his, but that night Anna Nicole Smith was sitting across from Stern in his small studio, and at one time, we had been among her biggest fans.

Stern was being particularly smutty. His commentary was lascivious, his thoughts ugly, his so-called humor characteristically straight out of the gutter. Yet there was something *un*characteristic about Stern that night, something unsettling.

Howard Stern, who normally wouldn't create a blip on the Sensitivity Scale, was trying to be kind to Anna.

It was clear to anyone watching that she was higher than a kite on something, maybe heroin—which we had been told was her new drug of choice—and almost certainly cocaine, an old favorite. Her speech was slurred, her eyes barely open. Stern knew it, too, and made gentle (for him) hints at her condition. She gave, in political parlance, a "nondenial denial" about her physical state, but her flat and dull tone belied the words. She spoke just above a whisper.

While Stern would never stop the interview—he makes his living pandering to the ugly side of the world, after all—he did wear cotton gloves for a while. It wasn't like him. He was showing pity. Can you imagine being pitied by Howard Stern?

In only a few years, Anna Nicole Smith has gone from waitress in a fried chicken restaurant to international media darling, from *Playboy* centerfold to grieving widow of a multimillionaire, from a reed-thin high school dropout to the symbol of overripe voluptuousness.

The journey has been recorded on the front pages of newspapers all over the world, on talk shows, on the big screen, in the courtrooms. What the world has seen has caused more than a few heads to shake in disbelief. What we have seen has made our heads shake in sorrow.

They say fame is a harsh taskmaster, and that has been never more true than with Anna Nicole Smith. But fame alone didn't bring Anna to that seat across from Howard Stern. Like us all, she has some control of her own fate. It's been her drive, her lust for power, money, and sex that has brought her to where she is today.

D'eva and I have been eyewitnesses to this bizarre passage. We met Anna in 1991 and contributed to her early successes. I took the Polaroid pictures that would lead her to a *Playboy* centerfold. D'eva held her hand, assured her that she didn't have to be frightened about showing that remarkable body of hers. I watched as my talented wife, a hair and makeup stylist, transformed an unsophisticated girl into a glittering jewel right there in the studio. I was the lucky guy who got to tell Anna that her dreams were about to come true.

But we've also been around to see the dark side. The drinking, the drug abuse, the reckless sex. We watched as she's turned her back on old friends, disregarded her own safety and the safety of her son, and spun her web of lies.

No writer, not even of the most grotesque Gothic tale, would have dared create Anna Nicole Smith. Her excesses, her bent on self-destruction, and disregard of acceptable social behavior go beyond the realm of believability.

It would be easy to make fun of Anna, but we can't. Maybe it's a case of "we knew her when," but we did—and we liked her then.

—Eric Redding
July 1996

Chapter 1

*T*exas is a state of contradictions and contrasts as big as its map. It is Black Lexuses and valet parking in Dallas and rifle racks and six-packs in El Paso. It is Silicon Valley-Southwest in Austin and cotton picking in Lubbock.

It embraces the sprawl of Houston with its 1,630,000 inhabitants and the backwater of Mexia, with the little more than 6,300 people within its boundaries.

So it is little wonder that Anna Nicole Smith sprang from Texas—Houston and Mexia in particular. For she, too, is a mix of contradictions, contrasts, and is big, like the state's map. Her overboard flamboyance, outrageous ambition, and unbounded self-indulgence is quintessentially Texas. Which isn't to say that everyone and everything there comport themselves in such a fashion.

However, it would be hard to imagine Anna Nicole Smith as a product of Missouri or Massachusetts. It had to be Texas, and Texas it was.

*D*espite Anna Nicole Smith living at the tail end of the twentieth century when record-keeping has reached a near–art form, one of the few things that is agreed upon about her background is that she was born on November 28, 1967, in Houston, as Vickie Lynn Hogan. From that point on, details get a little murky and change depending on who's doing the telling.

Some of the confusion may arise from her mother Virgie's predilection for men named Donald. Vickie Lynn's father was Donald Hogan, to whom Virgie may or may not have been married. Virgie was married to a Donald Hart and goes by that last name. There were three siblings—Shauna, who hasn't spoken to her sister for years; FBI agent David; and Donald, who is described by some family members as "retarded" and presently resides in a Huntsville prison for kidnapping.

Another reason for confusion is Vickie's occasional insistence that Virgie is not her mother. Over the years, Vickie has told more than one person that Virgie's younger sister, Kay Beall, was really her mother and not her aunt. Vickie would underscore this contention by calling Kay, "Mother."

This wishful thinking probably arose from the tension between Vickie and Virgie, who never got along well. Vickie would make claims of abuse such as being handcuffed to her bed so she couldn't sneak out at night. This story has some plausibility given that Virgie Hart has been a deputy sheriff in Harris County—which takes in Houston—for the past twenty years. But family members don't give the allegations much credence.

"Virgie was a good mother," Kay Beall says. "But you can't talk to her about anything. All my kids can talk to me no matter what. Even if it was about sex or what. If they need something, they can talk to me about it. I wasn't just their mother, I was their friend."

Kay Beall has another, somewhat stranger, explanation for Vickie's contention she was Kay's child.

When Kay was ten, she lived with her sister and Donald Hogan, and she claims that Hogan raped her. "That's why Vickie always thought that maybe I got pregnant. I couldn't get pregnant. I was still a child. But she would always try to make herself believe...that I was her mother. That I gave up the baby to Virgie."

Of course, in recent years as Anna Nicole Smith, Vickie has been telling people there's a chance she is Marilyn Monroe's baby. (Monroe died in 1962, five years before Vickie was born.) "Was she spaced out?" Kay Beall asked when she heard this story. "Someone's messing with her head. I saw Virgie have that baby. That's Virgie's baby."

Vickie Lynn was a student at Durkee Elementary School and Aldine Intermediate School in Houston, before moving to Mexia to attend high school and live with Kay Beall full time, although she had been a frequent visitor when she was younger. Kay Beall told *People* magazine, "She used to come over and stay with me and clean my house. I'd give her five dollars of my food stamps to let her go to the store and buy some candy." As part of Anna Nicole Smith's dirt-poor persona, stories are told of her stealing toilet paper from a local restaurant because Kay couldn't afford to buy any.

Mexia, as noted earlier, isn't much of a town. "Dusty" is the adjective used most frequently to describe it. Its main street is usually empty, and its movie theater has been converted into one of the town's twenty churches. If you're employed, it's most likely at the state home for the retarded.

Mexia, situated halfway between Interstates 35 and 45, some ninety miles south of Dallas, did have a brush with prosperity. It was once oil-rich, but that was long ago.

It was also the site of the largest World War II internment camp in Texas, where prisoners from Rommel's Afrika Corps sweltered in the sun behind twin rows of barbed wire.

Mexia's other claim to fame comes in the form of Ray Rhodes, former defensive coach of the Super Bowl champions San Francisco Forty-niners and later head coach of the Philadelphia Eagles.

In the midsixties, Rhodes was one of the outstanding athletes in southeast Texas, enough to make him popular in any small Texas town. He was great on the football field, the basketball court, and running track at Dunbar, an all-black high school in Mexia.

To come in compliance with federal desegregation rulings, Texas set up a "Freedom of Choice" plan. Students, black or white, could choose which schools they wished to attend. Interesting concept, but in practice it meant the white kids stayed in the white schools, and the black kids in the black schools.

The head football coach at the white Mexia High School persuaded Rhodes's father to transfer his son. Because Ray Rhodes went to Mexia High School, other black students followed. The integration of Mexia High was one of the trouble-free exceptions in the Deep South. "I can safely say that without Ray's leadership, things would not have gone as smoothly as they did," said Glenn McGuire, a Mexia math teacher.

Ray Rhodes as town celebrity would be a hard act to follow for anyone. Vickie Lynn/Anna Nicole would never come close to filling the town with similar pride.

Nevertheless, Anna Nicole Smith has deemed Mexia her "hometown," despite having lived there only a few years. Being nationally associated with Anna Nicole Smith today would seem to be an honor many residents of Mexia could live without. As Bob Wright, the editor of the *Mexia Daily News*, has put it with admirable diplomacy, "She's definitely adopted the town more than the town adopted her."

At Mexia High School, Vickie went by the name of Nikki and Cricket and was not in the running for Miss Popularity.

"She was just so common," a former classmate sniffed.

"I'll tell you one thing," another Mexia resident said, "she's not home grown."

"A nerd" was how her cousin Melinda described Vickie in high school. (Vickie/Anna sometimes refers to Melinda as her "niece," further confusing her family tree.)

As Anna Nicole Smith on her *Playboy* video, Vickie admitted that "I wasn't very popular in high school." However, she attributed that to her being flat-chested.

Vickie's advanced education ended in a fistfight with another student and expulsion. At seventeen, she went to work at Jim's Krispy Fried Chicken. When Vickie wasn't taking orders from customers and working in the kitchen, she was watching baby-faced Billy Smith, a sixteen-year-old cook.

"He paid no attention to me," she remembered, "and it drove me crazy. And I chased him and chased him and finally got him and married him." That was in April 1985.

It didn't take long before the marriage went sour. "He was really nice to me when we were dating, but then we got married. I wasn't allowed to go out of the house or go to the store...He was so jealous." His jealousy, according to Vickie, was punctuated by his fists. She says she thought having a baby might save the marriage or at least make things better. But the arrival of her son, Daniel, didn't signal a fairy-tale ending—at least not with Billy Smith.

"I stayed in the relationship for two years," she said. "I was so naive." Years later, Billy denied the abuse. He says that only once "I kicked her and she fell out of bed. I didn't hit her. I guess she was looking for an excuse to get out of the marriage."

Which is apparently what she got. Packing the few belongings she had, Vickie Lynn, her six-month-old baby, and her ambitions set off for the Big Time—Houston.

Chapter 2

*J*ouston. 1987. A great place for a great big beautiful doll with ambitions that went beyond frying chicken.

Dallas was a town of pretensions, a banking city where no one jaywalks. Houston was wide open, a boom-or-bust oil town, where each new skyscraper tried to outdo the last one. It was a place, as writer Mimi Swartz put it, of "big deals and big deeds, where self-invention has achieved the status of religion."

Vickie Lynn Hogan Smith was ready and more than willing to reinvent herself. Having dumped her husband and with a six-month-old baby in tow, Vickie did what any good red-blooded American girl would do—she moved in with Mama. Why either Vickie or Virgie, based on their acrimonious history, would think they could spend quality time together is anyone's guess.

The room-mating didn't last long and was highlighted by constant arguing. Vickie then packed up, leaving baby Daniel with Virgie, and moved into a trailer park with Deborah Hopkins, a hairdresser she knew. Hopkins was the one friend that Vickie would stick with through the years. She was the one who changed Vickie's hair color from the unremarkable shade of mouse-brown to traffic-stopping platinum. (Although as Anna Nicole, Vickie would often insist that was the color that sprang from her gene pool.)

There was still the problem of putting food on the table and clothes on her back. Vickie tried waitressing at a Red Lobster, but it didn't take a rocket scientist—of which Houston has many—to figure out that minimum wages and minimum tips would not finance the good times and excitement that she was craving.

What was a girl with little education and few marketable skills to do? If she was good-looking, which Vickie undeniably was, and willing, which Vickie proved unquestionably to be, you hit the topless bar circuit.

In Houston there exists a world that could send the Christian Coalition's Ralph Reed into a perpetual hissy fit. It is what the locals call "titty bars." Some are dark, sleazy, and only a cut above a truck stop. They are the kind of place that might make you send your clothes to be fumigated after spending a couple of minutes in them. The dancers who gyrate near-nude on the stage or practically in the customers' laps are often hard looking, as if from too much drugs, booze, and boyfriend abuse.

In 1987, at the other end of the titty bar spectrum was Rick's Cabaret. It boasted a faux-mansion decor with chandeliers and carpeting, good food and liquor, and dancers who were truly beautiful. But more than that, the women had that *Playboy* aura—the girl next door, that is if the girl next door was gorgeous and willing to drop her clothes for a room full of ogling men. These women exuded enough of a wholesome image that when it was reported that some showed up with their college course schedule to coordinate it with their dancing schedule, the story actually sounded plausible.

Rick's was the brainchild of Dallas Fontenot, who had operated run-of-the mill topless joints around Houston for years. He took over the lease of a disco that had hung on after Gloria Gaynor stopped getting air time, and he sought to fill a void. He wanted to create a "gentleman's club," a place for guys with Volvos in the driveways and nice dividend checks at the end of the quarter, guys who wanted to be *in* topless bars but not be seen entering or leaving them.

Fontenot succeeded. Rick's rose above being a mere titty bar. It was a place where celebrities—men primarily—flocked when they were in town or wanted a night on the town. Country western star George Strait. Warren Moon, the former Houston Oiler quarterback. Actor Michael Caine. Orenthal James Simpson, in his prepariah days. If an object of the paparazzi's attention didn't want to draw any, there were private rooms from which the customer could watch the dancers. Corporate memberships were sold with the promise that "We'll do everything in our power to make your next business deal your best business deal."

Vickie Lynn Smith started out at a club somewhere in the middle of the topless hierarchy, a place called the Executive Suites, which had no connection, corporate or otherwise, to the hotel chain of the same name.

The now-defunct Executives Suites was on the city's north side, conveniently near Houston International Airport. It catered to out-of-town businessmen and even provided limo service to the airport and nearby hotels.

Its manager, Terry Allen, remembers Vickie Lynn as being "fresh-looking" without the tough edge of a veteran. "I could tell she had a lot of potential...as she certainly was a pretty girl."

She was pretty enough that the club used her in one of its brochures. What Vickie wasn't enough of was endowed. She was a big girl at five feet eleven inches and between 160 and 180 pounds, big everywhere except where it counted in the topless bars. Which was one reason she worked the day shift, the time relegated for those were not so pretty or were flat chested or overweight.

Vickie wasn't going to let any shortcomings hold her back. Soon after being hired, she approached another dancer, Terri Cobble, a brunette with long straight hair who favored guys with leather jackets and motorcycles. She wanted Terri to teach her "how to dance seductively and give the men what they wanted," Terri recalls. "Vickie was a very quick learner and really became quite a seductive dancer in a hurry."

It wasn't long before Vickie had a following of regulars and was making more than $200 a day. Not being much of a money manager, she asked Terry Allen to set aside some of her earnings. Vickie had realized the truth of the topless business—the bigger the breasts, the bigger the tips—and she was saving for plastic surgery.

Despite the money she was bringing in, Vickie's nest egg didn't grow much. She kept asking for withdrawals from Terry Allen, with different excuses for why she needed the money. The real reason was probably that having a good time was becoming more expensive as Vickie was discovering new ways to have one. At some point, she added pills and drugs to her intake of alcohol. Wally Rodriguez, the hairstylist–makeup artist at Rick's Cabaret, says that "while Vickie would go do her dances and talk to her customers, I would have to hold her drugs for her, so she would not lose them. Her favorite drug or pill that she liked to take was Xanax [a popular prescription tranquilizer]...and boy, did she devour those...she lived on them. She used to keep them all in a Baggie and carry them around in...whatever."

According to Wally, Vickie was embarrassed by the size of her feet and would buy shoes that were too small. She would then turn to Wally for ministrations. "A lot of times when I was massaging her feet, she had taken so many Xanax and drank so much alcohol, that she would just pass out ... right there with her feet in my hand." He had seen Vickie many times so "messed-up," she could barely hold up her head.

Vickie's good time didn't stop with drugs and alcohol. Sex was added to the mixture, uninhibited, unrestrained, almost out-of-control sex. It might be argued that working where she did led to the wild behavior. Or Vickie Lynn might have been attracted to the topless bars because she could get away with it there. In either case, people began to take note that Vickie's erotic exhibitionism was not confined to the stage.

One such person was the deejay at Executive Suites, Randy Default. While it's true, a dancer needs to stay in the good graces of the guy who plays the music—what he chooses can make her look bad or good—Vickie carried it a step further. Default called Vickie a "carpet muncher" because she would drop to her knees in the deejay booth, the tune saloon, to perform oral sex on him.

She didn't seem to mind if other people were around. Mitchell White, an ex-manager of Executive Suites, says that he was witness to Vickie on her knees in the tune saloon. He also has said that Vickie would take her clients to dark corners of the club if she thought it might help to get more money from them. She loved to talk "baby talk" to well-paying regulars, he says.

*T*he topless bars were a circuit. Women didn't dance exclusively at one club. By 1988 Vickie—who went by the stage names of either Robyn and Nikki—had gotten good enough to get a day gig at Rick's. Her weight and size-A bra precluded working the more lucrative night shift. Still, she was beautiful enough for Dallas Fontenot to choose her for Rick's 1989 calendar.

The shoots were set up in the woods of East Texas. Fontenot had a long Lincoln Continental "loaded with a bar with champagne and booze and cameras and the works" so that the models could get "all fired up" on the way. It was on the drives that Fontenot noticed Vickie's interest in the other women. "She never did, at that time, any kind of sexual deals with the girls on film," Fontenot recalls, "just in the car...hugging and kissing and things like that."

He also remembers that despite the drinking, Vickie could still perform for the camera. She was a natural. "I always told her that she was great. She would make it in *Penthouse* and *Playboy* big time."

Because of her breast size, Fontenot shot her full length from the back, wearing nothing but boots and a dimple. He thought enough of the pictures that he sent them to *Penthouse*, but nothing came of it. "They weren't looking for big-boned women. Tall, big women. Especially tall, big women with no tits."

The breast size was a definite job liability. However, Houston was the right place to be if you wanted implants; it was practically the birthplace of silicone surgery.

Women through the ages have sought ways to enlarge their breasts and have allowed such varied substances as ivory and paraffin to be shoved into their bodies. The Japanese were the first to use silicone when women there wanted to be more attractive to American servicemen after World War II. The method used in this early silicone surgery was straight injection. It was not terribly successful. Even if the patient didn't get sick, the silicone had a tendency to wander or even harden, and the eventual results were less than aesthetically pleasing.

In the early sixties, two doctors at Houston's Baylor University College of Medicine, where Michael de Bakey did his pioneer work in heart surgery, wanted to create their own medical history by developing a successful, safe breast augmentation procedure. One was Thomas Cronin, a Baylor professor of plastic surgery who had established a reputation working with burn victims and hand injuries. The other was his resident, Frank Gerow.

It was Gerow who came up with the breakthrough idea one day at a blood bank. It was there that he saw blood being stored in plastic bags instead of the standard glass bottle. Why not put silicone into pliant plastic bags and implant them subcutaneously into a woman's breasts? In that way, the silicone wouldn't set out for destinations unwanted and would feel natural to the touch. Hence, the silicone-gel implant was born.

The doctors wrote at the time, "For some years now, at least in the United States, women have been bosom conscious. Perhaps this is due in large measure to the tremendous amount of publicity which has been given to some movie actresses blessed with generous-sized breasts. Many women with limited development of the breasts are extremely sensitive about it, apparently feeling that they are less womanly and therefore, less attractive. While most such women are satisfied, or at least put up with 'falsies,' probably all of them would be happier if, somehow, they could have a pleasing enlargement from within."

The implants were touted as absolutely safe and would last as long as the rest of woman's body did. "They're as harmless as water," Gerow would say more than once.

Breast jobs became the fashion for Houston ladies. And not only for those who lived in the ultra-tony River Oaks section of town. Secretaries and housewives were saving their pennies until they, too, could afford to increase their bra size by one or two cups—C and D being the most requested.

According to other dancers, one way Vickie was adding to her income was by accompanying clients to their cars and giving them blowjobs in the backseat for $25 or $50. Kimberleigh Graham, who knew her from Rick's, said she witnessed Vickie's second career on several occasions. When Beth Douglas was waitressing at a club where Vickie danced, she would always refer her clients to Vickie because Vickie was known as a "party girl" who was willing to party in the parking lots.

Through whatever means, Vickie put together enough money for her first breast augmentation. Of course, according to her version of history—as it has been repeated in numerous periodicals—her remarkable breast size was an act of god. She claims that during her pregnancy, she ballooned to 200 pounds. After Daniel was born, she lost the weight everywhere except in her chest.

Vickie didn't stop at one operation, however. Unhappy with the first one, she had a second, but there were complications and an infection. One of her breasts had to be drained which left her temporarily lopsided. Nicole Alexander met Vickie in 1989 after the first rounds of surgery. Alexander feels the original augmentations "looked better than the one she has now. Because they didn't screw up her nipples and all that. They [the breasts] weren't as big."

But Vickie, apparently wasn't satisfied. She wanted her breasts even larger and her nipples smaller. Alexander suggested she see Dr. Gerald Johnson, something of a legend even in a community of many plastic surgeon legends. In 1986 Dr. Johnson held what he called "Grand Teton Days." "The most surgeries we did in one day was seventeen," he told *Texas Monthly* magazine. In tribute to the many millions of dollars he earned from that particular part of the female anatomy, Dr. Johnson had a swimming pool built in the shape of a breast. The hot tub served as the nipple.

According to Suzy Pfardresher, a Houston pharmaceutical and medical supply saleswoman, Vickie's augmentation was unusual in that Dr. Johnson implanted not one but two 450 cc silicone sacks in each breast, one on top of the other. The result was a size 42DD bust, practically putting her breasts in a different zip code from the rest of her body.

Now this Vickie liked. When Guadalupe Castellano met her, she remembers being "... in awe of her beauty." She was also in awe of the size of Vickie's breasts. Lupe was thinking of getting her own implants and finally asked Vickie if she could feel hers.

"Feel them babies all you want," Vickie told her. "You're looking at $14,000 worth of work here. Hell, I could have bought myself a truck for what these damn things cost."

Actually it was a car, according to Nicole Alexander. "Some guy she was dating put out eight thousand for the boob job, because he was going to buy her a car. Instead, she had him pay for the tits."

Vickie continued to date her married benefactor, Alexander said, "until the money ran out."

Vickie and her new breasts made their way through the topless circuit. She worked intermittently at Rick's, although the day manager took exception to her drinking. Dallas Fontenot says she was " a real roller...a party type girl. She'd get drunk and drink, raise hell."

Vickie worked the Landing Strip, Legg's, Baby O's, but Gigi's Cabaret would end up being the most important club for Vickie's future.

Gigi's was a dark and grungy club complete with a pole for the dancers to entwine themselves around and slide seductively up and down. The main action was downstairs, but customers could request private table dancing in an upstairs room.

Donna Scanlin was a dancer whose career ended after three days at Gigi's. She was asked to table dance upstairs by a man she didn't know. "At Gigi's it's known that the upstairs is pretty risky compared to doing a table dance downstairs...I could kind of tell that he really wanted a lot more than I wanted to give."

When Donna turned him down, the guy wanted to know who would go upstairs with him. Being new at the club, Donna wasn't sure but when she asked around, she was told to get Vickie. "So later on I ended up going upstairs...to do a table dance for some-one I knew, and Vickie was up there dancing for that man...Her G-string was pulled over to the side, and he was fondling her. I actually hurried up and finished my table dance and went down-stairs. I never went back to Gigi's and danced again. That's the last time I ever danced."

Gigi's is where Vickie became close friends with April Story Richardson, although they had met earlier. The first time April "laid eyes on her, she was on her back with her legs spread on a stage" at the Landing Strip.

The women danced together at Gigi's. "The management real-ly liked us, and the owners, too. We got to come and go as we please. Nobody ever told us no and we knew we could never get fired." This was lucky for Vickie since her drinking and drugging and sexual forays were stretching the limits of even the no-holds-barred world of the topless clubs. The woman was out of control, even when it came to those she considered friends.

Take the time she asked April and her husband to drive her to the airport. A customer Vickie had met only three hours earlier wanted her in Dallas. April thought the rendezvous was a bad idea, especially since Vickie was drunk and getting drunker in the backseat with something she'd bought for the road. That's when the ride went from bad to bizarre. "Before we got to the airport," April says, "she had leaned over the driver's seat and taken her right hand and grasped my husband between the legs as I sat in the passenger seat. Of course, my eyes are bulging out at this time. I couldn't believe this. I didn't know to be mad or to laugh. It was just one of those situations." April's husband didn't say anything. "He just kind of stares into space." When they pulled up at departures, Vickie hopped out as if nothing untoward had taken place.

That was the beginning of the end of April's marriage. After April split with her husband, Vickie moved in along with two cats, two toy poodles, and Gizmo, the cockatiel. It was only then that April began to notice what half of Houston already knew—Vickie liked more than just guys. "She made comments to me about former lovers she had and they were girls." One even had had a likeness of Vickie tattooed on her back.

If anything, Vickie preferred women. In paying a high compliment to a male boyfriend, Clay Spires, she said he used his mouth like a woman in lovemaking.

Nicole Alexander said, "She was more partial to women, because she would get money from men and buy stuff for her girlfriends." According to Nicole, Vickie mostly dated dancers, but she also went regularly to a Houston lesbian bar, Bacchus.

Lupe Castellano said she had heard through the club scene that

Vickie mostly "just preferred woman," although that didn't preclude her from bringing men home or "even couples." Most of the women she'd seen Anna with were surprisingly unattractive and very butch. Vickie needed the spotlight, and she didn't want competition.

Another dancer, Nikki Mizzell, had seen pictures of Vickie with a lover—a woman who had been with both Nikki and Vickie. The photographs showed the two women in the nude with Vickie snorting a line of cocaine from the other's stomach.

Cocaine. Xanax. Alcohol. Downers like Ecstasy. Gifts for girlfriends. Not even the side trips to Vegas with three other dancers and four wealthy businessmen—especially when the men lost their mortgage checks at the tables and stiffed the women—could cover Vickie's appetites. So it was a very lucky day when the octogenarian multimillionaire decided to have lunch at Gigi's Cabaret. Had he chosen a more posh dining setting, Tony's or the River Oaks Country Club, J. Howard Marshall II might have never met Vickie Lynn Smith, which would have left a lot of future tabloid pages to be filled.

Chapter 3

J. Howard Marshall II is as much a product of Texas as Vickie Lynn Hogan although their beginnings were far apart, both in physical distance and social standing.

J. Howard came from a prominent Quaker family that could boast of having in its tree John Marshall, the preeminent fourth chief justice of the Supreme Court who established through his interpretations of the constitution the power of that court.

J. Howard's grandfather was in the steel business. In 1902, three years before J. Howard was born in Philadelphia, the grandfather sold his company to Andrew Carnegie for the then-staggering sum of eighteen million dollars.

As a boy, J. Howard followed the Quaker tradition of addressing adults as thee and thou. But by the time he was ready to enter college, the family fortune had been dissipated. J. Howard, as

determined in his way as Vickie Lynn was in hers, did not let
adversity stand in his way. He had already proven an inner strength
when doctors said he would never walk again after a bout with
typhoid fever when he was twelve. His mother burned his crutch-
es and Marshall eventually walked—although a limp stayed with
him for the rest of his life.

Marshall worked his way through both Haverford College, a
prestigious Quaker school on the prestigious Main Line outside of
Philadelphia, and then Yale Law School. While working on the
Yale Law Review in 1931, Marshall took an assignment that determined the direction of the rest of his life. He went out to research
an article in the Oklahoma oil fields. The article must have been
impressive because two years later Secretary of the Interior Harold
Ickes asked him to investigate the rising acrimony between regula-
tors of the Texas Railroad Commission and oil producers accused
of exceeding extraction allowances.

Marshall had to dodge a few bullets while in Texas, but it was
worth it for the contacts he made there. During World War II, he
was appointed chief counsel of the Petroleum Administration for
the War. In 1944, he left public service and set out to make money
as a consummate dealmaker. He helped Ashland Oil become a
major player, and later was instrumental in the expansion of Signal
Oil and Gas.

But it wasn't until 1961 that this tiny man with big ears and a
bigger voice found his true home—where someone who had written the regulations in Washington could make them work for his
and his partners' profit. Marshall moved to Houston. There, after
a stint with Allied Chemical, he merged his resources with Fred
Koch's huge energy firm in what he called in his autobiography,
Done in Oil, "the best deal I ever made." That best deal, with him
eventually controlling 8 percent of Koch Industries, would land

him on *Forbes* magazine's 1991 list of the 400 richest people in the United States, with an estimated net worth of $400 million. However, there were those who scoffed at the estimate, saying Marshall's true worth was closer to three billion.

The move to Houston brought on domestic changes for Marshall, as well. He ditched his wife of thirty years, Eleanor Pierce, writing in his autobiography that "she never really understood my driving passion for the oil business." The divorce didn't sit well with his younger son, Pierce, but maintaining warm relations with his family never seemd to be a driving ambition of Marshall's. In the 1980s he had a serious falling out with son John Marshall III over the attempt to take Koch Industries public. Papa Marshall was against it and bought out his son's interest for $8 million, which apparently did not assuage his son's bad feelings.

Having gotten rid of wife number one, Marshall married number two a few months later. From all outward appearances, the union with Bettye Bohanon, who was nicknamed "Tiger," was a happy one. Tiger worked with Marshall in the oil business for some twenty years until she developed Alzheimer's disease. Marshall found himself virtually a widower although his wife was still alive.

Then, in 1982, according to *Texas Monthly,* he "...landed at the Houston Hobby Airport and driving home, I thought, well, maybe if I had a drink I'd feel better, so I stopped at some little place that I didn't realize what I was getting into. It was a strip joint—or as the boys call it now—a titty bar. And I walked in and Lady was there. She was one of the strippers."

Jewell Dianne Walker, bosomy, tall, leggy, had only been in Houston two years when Marshall spotted her. She had barely arrived in 1980 when her fourth husband returned to Georgia, leaving Lady with three kids. She went through a series of low-paying jobs—receptionist, waitress, whatever she could get—until, at the age of forty-two, she took to the stage at the Chic Lounge, dancing topless.

To say that Lady Walker was a character would be a gross understatement. She had panache, Southern charm, and amusing tales of affairs with the likes of Elvis Presley and Pete Rose.

Marshall liked what he saw that first night and asked for a private dance. He must have been even more impressed for within days he bought Lady a Cadillac El Dorado, a new house—complete with furniture—a diamond ring, and the list got longer and longer. By all evidence, he was genuinely smitten with Lady. He sent her love notes along with the gifts. One read, "To love and be loved—to man who has dedicated his life to his work, this is truly life's great experience."

The one glitch in the romance, however, was Bettye, his ill wife. Marshall wrote Lady's mother that "I would marry her this afternoon...if I were free and she would have me. I cannot leave an ill wife to whom I have been married. I think it might kill her and I would feel guilty for the rest of my life. Perhaps a time will come."

Because of Bettye, Marshall and Lady entered into an accommodating arrangement. The mores of Houston society deemed it improper to be seen with your mistress in the evening, but taking her to lunch was no problem. So three days a week for ten years, Marshall and Lady lunched in the best places in Houston. Lady made the most of it. She dressed with a such flair, it was impossible not to notice her—hats, scarves, and plenty of jewels. She and Marshall practically held court at their tables, with him telling amusing stories of his Washington days and her just being flat-out charming.

Marshall often would unobtrusively pass blank checks to Lady at the table. (It was later alleged by Marshall's son Pierce that she was spending one hundred thousand dollars a month.) Once he made the mistake of giving them to her openly for all to see. "Put it in my purse. Don't just hand it across the table," she instructed him. She didn't get the nickname Lady for nothing.

By Marshall's account the sexual part of their relationship was over, by mutual consent, when he was eighty-three. According to *Texas Monthly* writer Mimi Swartz, Lady "intended to get on with her life as long as Marshall remained married," but that she did plan to marry him one day. "He may have been old," Swartz wrote, "but he was entertaining and he knew how the world worked, and he was more than willing to share his knowledge with her."

Marshall continued to indulge her expensive tastes—she was said to have had a jeweler on retainer who was paid $25,000 a month. One house wasn't enough for her. Marshall bought her a second, larger one. It was extravagantly furnished and appointed. Lady's swimming pool, with her name in tiles on the bottom, was designed by the man who had created Liberace's, famous for its piano shape.

One thing the house was lacking was Marshall. Lady ruled that "When I can set foot in his house as Mrs. Marshall, he can set foot in mine."

Lady filled the void in her houshould with a bodyguard-lover named Dale Clem, whom she showered with cars and diamonds and money. It is clear that Marshall knew of Clem's existence, but what later became a matter of legal contention was whether he was aware of their intimate relationship.

Marshall did write a letter to his son Pierce about this time instructing that in the event of his death, Pierce should "take care

of [Lady] in any way she may need, financially and in all ways...
I'm completed obligated to take care of her!"

Then Lady and Marshall started having tiffs over money—
including her liability for taxes on the gifts that Marshall had given
her over the years without reporting them to the IRS. He went so
far as to close an account without telling her. To her mortification,
she bounced checks all over town, but he eventually covered them.

It wasn't only Marshall Lady was fighting with. There were
fallings-out with friends and family. Lady was not living up to her
nickname. Some of her ill-temper may have been due to reaching
that iffy age for mistresses. Even when your paramour has thirty
years on you, turning fifty can be an awkward passage. So Lady did
what many women in a similar position do. In 1991 she signed up
for cosmetic surgery.

The night before the operation, Lady updated her will. Her
$5.8 million estate consisted of what Marshall had given her, and
she was leaving that to her children. Except for a truck, a diamond
bracelet, and a poodle named Fancy that were to go to Clem.

Lady died on the operating table. The cause of death was listed as a congenital brain defect, although later rumors swirled
around about Lady's morphine pump having been tampered with.
Marshall gave her a grand burial complete with a copper casket.
But not long afterwards, he found out about Lady's will and over
lunch with Clem, he found out about Lady's sex life. To add to
Marshall's emotional trauma, in September, Bettye died.

In February 1992, Marshall sued Lady's heirs and some of her
friends in an attempt to retrieve every dime he'd ever spent on his
mistress. He had given those gifts to her, he contended, not her
kids and certainly not Dale Clem. Marshall was to testify that, "I
was blinded by love. I did more or less what she asked me to do,
and I don't make any bones about it, I was a damn fool. But men

in love do stupid things, and I was sure guilty." (Although it's been suggested that what he really was a damn fool about was transferring one million dollars worth of stock into Lady's name, a transaction which the Securities and Exchange Commission definitely frowned upon.)

Marshall claimed that Lady had given the appearance of loving him exclusively while all the time she was carrying on affairs with other men. He said that the gifts he had given her had been in trust only—Lady wasn't supposed to own them until his death. In fact, he claimed, she'd swindled him out of his fortune. All this, even though Lady was heard saying to him many times that as long as he was married, she would continue to see other men.

It was a particularly juicy legal brouhaha, which kept Houston amused for awhile. It was settled a year and half later with Marshall getting the lion's share of the estate. Lady's family didn't have the resources to keep on fighting.

What should not be overlooked in the timing of these events was Marshall, apparently a man of consistency, having ventured into another topless bar and having another tall, busty dancer catch his eye. And this time it was no Lady, it was Vickie Lynn Smith. According to not only Vickie, but others as well, this momentous encounter took place while Lady was still alive, making Marshall's cries of betrayal more than a bit hypocriticial.

Dan Manning, Marshall's driver, remembers that day at Gigi's Cabaret. Marshall had gone in for lunch, spotted Vickie, and was intrigued by her. He sent Manning to bring her over to the table so he could get a better look. He apparently liked what he saw. (This was post–Dr. Gerald Johnson.)

Dallas Fontenot says that Vickie was "the kind of girl you can sit down and talk to and she would sit down and talk to you for hours. She wasn't a hard hustler like some of the girls. They got their three-minute drinks, [and then it was] I got to be back up there dancing. She wasn't that kind of girl. She'd spend time with you. Especially if she thought her career could go places."

Talk she did. She told Marshall how she didn't really like to dance, but she had to in order to support her young son. This must have been deja vu to Marshall, still he wanted to help her out, Dan Manning recalls.

Helping her out took the form of $500 in cash here, then $1000 there, until it climbed to $2000.

Howard would melt when Vickie would start in with her baby talk, a ploy she used with many of her older customers. Manning says initially his employer would hand Vickie an envelope filled with money at those lunches, perhaps heeding Lady's admonition on etiquette, but that ritual soon ended when Vickie stopped all pretense and just removed the bills from Marshall's wallet.

According to some of those who were around at the time, there was a quid pro quo involved. April Richardson, for one, remembers one afternoon Vickie told her that Marshall had given her some money and expected a blow job in return. She had to hurry up and do it, so she could get more money.

"[Marshall] was very old," April said. "Sometimes he was very rude, very abrupt. We all put up with him because he was so rich. [Vickie] didn't seem to mind going out to him. She liked him. And he sure liked her."

But at this point in Vickie's life, Marshall was just another guy giving her money. She had more important things on her agenda.

Chapter 4

Vickie Lynn Smith had ambitions beyond shaking her assets on the stage of Gigi's Cabaret and picking up extra income in the parking lot. She, after all, had written on her April page of Rick's calendar, "My one ambition and goal in life is to be a high-fashion model."

With that in mind, Vickie went to the Intermedia Modeling Agency/Page Parkes School of Modeling. Vickie was advised to darken her hair, lose weight, change her image, and then she might be accepted into the modeling school—for a fee, of course. Vickie didn't have the money.

Her new boyfriend, a bodybuilder named Clay Spires, suggested she follow up on an ad they had spotted in the Houston edition of *Health and Fitness* magazine. It was an ad we ran. We were recruiters for Playboy Enterprises and were looking for potential Playmates of the Month. When we found young—they had to be at least eighteen years old—women with potential, we'd have them fill out a standard one-page biography. Eric would take Polaroid test shots of them au naturel—in the nude and without makeup. We'd send the pictures to the *Playboy* photography editors for evaluation.

Vickie called us in September, 1991, to ask for an appointment. She gave the impression she was only contacting us because Clay Spires insisted. Eric had to practically cajole her into making an appointment. He pointed out that the potential rewards were great, the risks few, so why not take a chance? Once she was convinced that the appointment would simply be an honest evaluation followed by some quick test shots, she set a time. It took three cancellations before she actually made it to the studio late in the afternoon of Saturday, September 7.

The first thing you noticed about Vickie Lynn Smith was invariably her size. There was a lot of her to notice, the five feet eleven inches, the 160 pounds, those outrageous 42DD-cup breasts. It was somewhat overwhelming. But once Eric got past the initial impression and really took a look at her, he realized he was looking at a truly beautiful woman.

Vickie had perfect skin and a stunning heart-shaped face with large eyes and a generous mouth. If you wanted to nitpick, there was a flaw, a small crease below her right eye that became marked when she smiled. But that's why airbrushing was invented. She was a complete stunner, even without a drop of makeup.

Vickie was very nervous at first, so Eric talked with her a while to give her a chance to relax a bit before the session.

She talked about Clay and Daniel, her son. Eric was surprised to learn she had made them wait downstairs in the car instead of bringing them to the studio. But he thought their presence might make her even more nervous. As it was, even the easiest topics seemed to fluster her, and finally she admitted that she was afraid of posing nude. "You can see everything so clearly!"

With a straight face, she said she never let any of her boyfriends see her naked. Lovemaking was strictly a lights-off affair. Eric had to play diplomat/psychiatrist, reassuring her that the session would go quickly and she would be nude only for a few minutes. Still she sat shaking in her chair. Eric felt sorry for her, there was something so childlike about her. She acted and sounded as if she had just gotten off the bus from a small town that hadn't had the benefit of a grammar teacher.

To get her mind off the shoot, Eric had her fill out the requisite one-page biography. It usually took a few minutes to answer the questions, but Vickie didn't understand several of them and asked more than once for clarification. Finally, after a half hour, she was done.

Under occupation, Vickie first wrote dancing, scratched it out, and then put modeling. However, she neglected to alter the phone number she gave for the original answer, that number being the direct line to Gigi's Cabaret. This oversight would come back to haunt her.

She wrote that her hobby was "Watching scary movies." That "horse back riding" was her sport or special activity. Under likes, she put, "Gentlemen who no [sic] how to treat a lady. Dislikes: "Cigeret [sic] smoke, bums with no jobs." Ambition: "To be in *Playboy* + model, actress."

In retrospect, the most incongruous response she gave was to About Men (Likes or Dislikes): "I don't like men who always talk about how much money they have." (Although in her defense, she probably didn't want to hear about the money, she merely wanted

·8

TENTATIVE FEATURE: _____
PHOTOGRAPHER: _____
EXACT DATE(S) AND LOCATION OF PHOTOGRAPHY: _____
_____

BIOGRAPHICAL INFORMATION

Legal Name: Vickie Smith
(Please print)
Home Address: 300 Woerner # 2117
No.   Street   City   State   Zip Code
Phone #: 5375670   Social Security #: _____
Place of Birth: Houston   Date of Birth: 11-28-67
Education: Mexia High
Current School Address & Phone # (If Applicable) _____
modeling
Occupation: ~~XXXXXXXXX~~   Business Phone #: 688 3401
Hobbies: watching scary movies
Sports or Special Activities: Horse back riding
Likes: Gentlemen who no how to treat a lady
Dislikes: Cigeret smoke, Bums with no jobs
Ambition: to be in playboy + model, Actress
About Men (Likes or Dislikes): I Don't like men who always talk about how much money they ha
Other Interesting Remarks About Yourself or Family: I have a 5 yr old son we been raising by myself and my mom is a very big help to me
Parent's Occupation(s): mother is a Deputy Sheriff

Height	Weight	Bust/Cup	Waist	Hips	Hair	Eyes	Shoe Size
5"11	140	42.DD	26	38	Blonde	Hazel	10

CLOSE FRIEND OR RELATIVE WHO CAN ALWAYS FIND YOU

Name: Virgie Hart   Phone #: _____
Area Code
Address: 8106
No.   Street   City   State   Zip Code
How Related: mother

to get it.) Under Other Interesting Remarks About Yourself or Family, she wrote "I have a 5 yr old son we been raising by myself and my mom is a very big help to me." Parent's Occupation(s): "mother is a deputy Sheriff."

And finally, she filled in these statistics: Height 5"11 [sic], Weight 140, Bust/Cup 42,DD, Waist 26, Hips 38, Hair Blonde, Eyes Hazel, Shoe Size 10.

With the excruciating process of completing the form over, Vickie went to the dressing room, where she was to remove all her clothes, put on a robe, and wait until the marks from her bra straps had disappeared.

This meant more time for talk and confidences. Vickie had a dream, a big one, she told Eric. And she was convinced that making the pages of *Playboy* would be the first big step toward that dream. She wanted to become the next Marilyn Monroe. Vickie was not the first blonde to wish that, nor would she be the last, but sitting across from her wrapped in a terry-cloth robe, with her perfect face and her lush curves, Eric could almost believe she had a shot.

Finally, it was show time. No more hesitation. If Vickie wanted to grace the pages of *Playboy*, the robe was going to have to come off. When it did, Eric could see she was an exceptional girl. His eyes went first to her breasts. And little wonder, they looked even larger in the nude. As a photographer for *Playboy*, Eric had seen many busty girls in his studio, but Vickie had outdone them all. However, on closer inspection, he was shocked to see that her breasts were scarred quite badly around the nipples and aureoles and that she had deep, long stretch marks that were going to be tough to hide with makeup.

Her breasts weren't the only thing that were out of the ordinary, especially for a woman who wanted to be a centerfold. She was big boned, with very large hands, arms, thighs, and an especially large derriere.

Most of the women that come in for *Playboy* photographs are thin, with toned bodies that are small and tight, even if the woman is tall. Not Vickie. She was a Rubens painting, zaftig, full, and exuberant. She was unlike anyone Eric had seen before.

What came next was standard procedure. First, Eric took about a dozen Polaroids that included a closeup of her face, a beside-the-swimming-pool pose, full-length shots, front and back. The photographs were taken against a plain background without any props. Her hair and makeup were not professionally done, and there was no effort to mask flaws. The *Playboy* editors want to get a good look at the girls at this stage. No distractions.

When the session ended, Vickie was heading back to the dressing room when D'eva got her first glimpse of her. She studied Vickie with an artist's eye. "God, you have a beautiful face," she said. "That face is going to make you a lot of money."

Of course, Vickie was thrilled to hear this. She thanked D'eva and went to change into her street clothes. D'eva repeated her assessment to Eric. That face was going to make Vickie a fortune. Her skin was clear and beautiful, there was a youthful look about her. Very lovely, very innocent. The illusion was spoiled somewhat when Vickie returned encased in a Spandex minidress and spiked heels.

Vickie, naturally, wanted to know when she might hear something from *Playboy*. Eric told her it usually took a week or so. She thanked us and left.

Eric sent the Polaroids to *Playboy* photo editor Linda Kenney, and her boss, Marilyn Grabowski. It took only three days for Linda Kenney to call back with instructions to do a *Playboy* Playmate Test on Vickie. The Polaroids are the first step in the screening process. They whet the editors' interest to see what the model can do on 35mm film, if she can come alive before the camera and project the look they want.

A *Playboy* Playmate Test (PMT) is usually a day photo shoot. The model is asked to show up with no makeup, clean hair, and loose-fitting clothes. Tight garments could mean lost time waiting for body marks to fade. The model's hair is then styled and makeup applied, usually by a licensed cosmetologist, which D'eva is, so Vickie agreed to use her for the session.

The PMT was scheduled for Monday, September 17. Only one day would be needed to do both the studio and outdoor shots. However, that Monday morning Vickie called to report that she'd had a boating accident the day before and that she had cuts and bruises all over her body.

Cuts and bruises are virtually impossible to cover with makeup, and it was agreed that the session would be postponed until she'd healed somewhat. Linda Kenney was not happy on being informed of the delay. She'd seen something in those first Polaroids, and she wanted the PMT done as quickly as possible.

Vickie finally came in for her PMT on Tuesday morning, October 2, 1991, alone, freshly scrubbed, and without makeup. D'eva took her into the salon area of the studio, where they quickly got into a discussion about skin types, hair styles, colors, and an overall approach to enhancing Vickie's beauty.

It was clear Vickie didn't know much about style. This was the second time we'd seen her, and once again she was wearing a skintight Spandex dress and five-inch heels.

At that time, we were unfamiliar with the topless dancing subculture and assumed that Vickie was dressed in what she naively thought was glamour garb. Being from that tiny town in Texas, it made sense that she wasn't sophisticated and that she would go overboard on makeup and overall flash. It was only later that we realized she wasn't the innocent flower she claimed to be. Her style was titty-bar chic, and she did everything she could to advertise her body, especially her breasts.

D'eva had other plans for her, however. She trimmed Vickie's hair and gave it a much softer look. As for makeup, D'eva astonished Vickie with her skill. It's quite possible that Vickie hadn't realized, until she looked at herself in that mirror, just how beautiful she really was. It was as if she'd been granted a wish by a fairy godmother. She was Cinderella. She was touched by D'eva's magic.

We left the studio and headed for the outdoor location. Vickie, both nervous and excited, didn't say a great deal. D'eva caught her looking at herself in the side mirror, glancing away, looking again.

Our destination was Sugar Land, an upscale subdivision on the southwest side of Houston. There was a small lake on the outskirts, one Eric had used as a backdrop before. Although it wasn't on a main thoroughfare, it wasn't isolated, and he cautioned Vickie that someone might see him taking the photographs. She would be nude, of course, and he asked her if that would be a problem. She assured him it would not.

Once there, we carried the equipment down to the lake, and Eric set up for the first shots. When it was time for her to disrobe, Vickie, instead of being shy as we expected, ducked under a tree and whipped off her dress. It was clear she was excited, and she wanted to be in front of the camera. Quite a change from the first session, when she'd literally trembled at the thought of being nude.

After D'eva touched her up and applied some body makeup, Vickie was ready. What Eric saw through that lens was something he'd never forget.

Vickie Lynn Smith *loved* the camera, and the camera loved her right back. She blossomed out there in Sugar Land. D'eva stood to the side, coaxing Vickie into different poses, but the student soon outpaced the teacher. She was a natural, a goddess. Eric had never seen anything quite like it. Vickie was a photographer's dream come true, and we knew this girl was going to make it.

All the reticence from the first session had disappeared, and Vickie showed herself to be quick, supple, clever. She surprised us over and over again with her verve and willingness to experiment.

The three of us were stoked by the time she got dressed. It was a thrilling day, filled with untold promise. When we drove to the next location, Vickie had buried all vestiges of shyness. She talked on and on about her dreams, about how she'd always wanted to be a *Playboy* centerfold, and how that was going to be her stepping-stone to acting. She was like a kid on Christmas, and we felt a little like Santa Claus.

The next set was our attorney's house where Vickie posed in front of his elegant brick fireplace: The shoot moved quickly, with no wrong turns. By the time we were through, we all felt the need to celebrate, and Eric made a quick trip to the liquor store. When he got back, D'eva and Vickie were more than ready to party, and the champagne cork popped to a chorus of cheers. We toasted the future, the fame, the money, the sheer excitement of it all.

Vickie really put away the bubbly. D'eva didn't think much of it at the time and certainly didn't realize that this was not the exception, but the rule. She just thought Vickie was a sweet kid from Mexia who was about to set the world on fire.

How were we to know that she'd lied on the biography? That the boating accident which had delayed the PMT had been a car accident, one that got her sued for personal injury because she rear-ended another vehicle while allegedly under the influence of alcohol? Or that the fresh-faced beauty with such endearing naivete had been a topless dancer and selling her favors for the past four years?

PLAYMATE DATA SHEET AND MODEL RELEASE

In the event you are selected as a Playmate of the Month for PLAYBOY Magazine, the information provided below will be essential for our story. All questions should be answered as fully and truthfully as possible, in your own handwriting.

LEGAL NAME __VICKIE LYNN SMITH__ AGE __23__

ADDRESS(Street) __300 W OERNER__ (City) __HOUSTON__ (State) __TX.__

PHONE (Home) __713-537-5670__ (Business) _____ ZIP CODE __77090__

NATIONAL EXTRACTION __UNITED STATES__

HEIGHT __6FT 5'11"__ WEIGHT __140 150__ EYE COLOR __HAZEL__ HAIR COLOR __BLONDE__

BUST __42 DD__ WAIST __26__ HIPS __38__

SWEATER SIZE __MEDIUM__ SKIRT SIZE __9__ DRESS SIZE __9__

BIRTH DATE __11-28-67__ PLACE OF BIRTH __HOUSTON__ MARITAL STATUS __S__

NUMBER OF CHILDREN, IF ANY __1__ AGES __5__

S.S.# _____ SHOE SIZE __10__

OTHER CITIES AND COUNTRIES IN WHICH YOU'VE RESIDED:

__MEXIA, TEXAS__ From 19 __82__ until 19 __88__

__(MY MOM + GRANDPARENTS ARE FROM__ From 19 ____ until 19 ____

__MEXIA - SO I HAVE LIVED THERE ON + OFF)__ From 19 ____ until 19 ____

FATHER'S NAME __DONALD HART__ OCCUPATION __———__

MOTHER'S NAME __VIRGIE HART__ OCCUPATION __DEPUTY ~~SUPER~~ SHERIF__

CITY AND STATE IN WHICH PARENTS RESIDE __HOUSTON, TX.__

IF UNMARRIED, DO YOU LIVE AT HOME? ____ ALONE? __✓__ WITH ROOMMATE(S) ____

HOW MANY BROTHERS __2__ AGES __18, 24__ SISTERS __1__ AGES __27__

IS THERE ANYTHING PARTICULARLY INTERESTING OR UNUSUAL ABOUT ANY MEMBERS OF YOUR

FAMILY? __MY MOTHER IS A POLICE OFFICER + HAS BEEN FOR 16 YEARS.__

GRAMMAR SCHOOL(S) __DURKEE ELEM.__ City, State __Hou, TX.__ 19__77__ to 19__82__

+ ~~XXXX~~ __ALDINE INT.__ City, State __Hou, TX.__ 19__82__ to 19__84__

HIGH SCHOOL(S) __MEXIA__ City, State __MEXIA, TX.__ 19__84__ to 19__86__

_____ City, State _____ 19___ to 19___

COLLEGE(S) __NA__ City, State _____ 19___ to 19___

_____ City, State _____ 19___ to 19___

COLLEGE MAJORS __NA__ DEGREES _____

OTHER SCHOOLS ATTENDED __PAGE PARKES__ City, State __HOUSTON__ 19__?__ to 19__?__

__MODELING SCHOOL__ City, State _____ 19___ to 19___

PLANS FOR CONTINUING YOUR EDUCATION _____ WHERE? _____

__?.__

_____

CURRENT OCCUPATION __MODELING / MOTHER__

NAME OF CURRENT EMPLOYER (Firm) __VARIOUS__ (City) __HOUSTON__

NATURE OF BUSINESS __MODELING__ EMPLOYED SINCE __?__

PREVIOUS EMPLOYERS (Firm name, city & state, how long employed and position):

(1) __BREAKFAST COOK__ __?__

_____

(2) _____

_____

CAREER AMBITIONS __TELEVISION + VIDEO MODELING —__
__LIKE MTV FOR INSTANCE__

PREVIOUS MODELING EXPERIENCE: Pin-up___ Nudes___ Fashion__✓__ Artist___ Other __ADVERTISING__

THEATRICAL EXPERIENCE: Stage___ Movies___ TV___ Nightclubs___ Other _____

TITLES OF PLAYS, MOVIES, TV SHOWS, NAMES OF NIGHTCLUBS __NA__

_____

HAVE NUDE OF SEMI-NUDE PHOTOGRAPHS OF YOU EVER BEEN PUBLISHED IN A MAGAZINE? _____
IF SO, GIVE NAME OF MAGAZINES(S) AND DATES(S) PUBLISHED __NA__

_____

HAVE YOU EVER POSED FOR NUDE OR SEMI-NUDE PHOTOGRAPHS OTHER THAN THE TEST SHOTS NOW
BEING TAKEN FOR PLAYBOY? __NO__ IF SO, WHEN AND FOR WHOM? _____

_____

DID YOU SIGN A MODEL RELEASE FOR THE PICTURES? _____ WERE YOU PAID? _____

The questions below will be most important in determining your picture story. Please give each question some thought before answering and give as much detail as possible.

DO YOU PLAN TO DO ANYTHING IN PARTICULAR WITH THE MONEY EARNED AS A PLAYMATE?

I WOULD LIKE TO TAKE MY AUNT WHO RAISED ME ON A CRUISE — ESPECIALLY SINCE SHE IS IN ILL-HEALTH. ALSO, I WOULD GET A CAR.

IF YOU COULD CHOOSE ONE PLACE IN THE WORLD TO VISIT, WHERE WOULD IT BE AND WHY?

I WOULD LOVE TO VISIT PARIS BECAUSE OF THE FASHIONS, BUT ALSO, I WOULD LOVE TO GO TO THE CAYMAN ISLANDS, BECAU

IF YOU COULD CHOOSE A CAREER FOR YOURSELF, WHAT WOULD IT BE AND WHY?

I LOVE THE SU

AN ACTRESS, BECAUSE I WOULD LIKE TO BE SEEN IN THE MOVIES.

IF YOU WERE TO DECIDE WHAT KIND OF A PICTURE STORY IS DONE ON YOU, HOW WOULD THE STORY GO? IN THE COUNTRY, WITH LOTS OF HORSES, HAY, AND COWBOYS — I LOVE COWBOYS.

WHO, IN THE ENTIRE WORLD, WOULD YOU LIKE TO MEET AND GET TO KNOW? WHY?

HULK HOGAN — BECAUSE HE'S FUNNY AND MAKES ME LAUGH.

PLEASE GIVE US AN EXAMPLE OF A TYPICAL DAY IN YOUR LIFE.

GET UP AND EAT BREAKFAST, TALK TO MY SO PREPARE FOR THE DAY... PHONE CALLS, ETC., WATCH TV.

WHAT DO YOU DO IN YOUR SPARE TIME? I LOVE TO RIDE HORSES AND WATCHING SCARY MOVIES!

WHAT WOULD YOU LIKE TO DO IF YOU HAD MORE TIME? I WOULD LIKE TO GO TO MEXIA AND SPEND MORE TIME WITH MY AUNT.

FAVORITE BOOKS I DON'T READ MUCH!

FAVORITE AUTHORS

FAVORITE MOVIES DRAMAS, SCARY MOVIES

FAVORITE TV SHOWS SIMPSONS

FAVORITE FOODS AND DRINKS I LOVE BIG RED + PASTA

FAVORITE KIND OF MUSIC COUNTRY

FAVORITE PERFORMERS GARTH BROOKS, KENNY ROGERS

FAMOUS MEN AND WOMEN YOU ADMIRE CHRISTIE BRINKLEY

WHY? BECAUSE SHE IS BEAUTIFUL + IS WHERE I WOULD LIKE TO BE.

YOUR PET PEEVES ARE I CANNOT STAND FOR A MAN TO ASK ME FOR PHONE CHANGE + NOT OPENING DOORS.

YOU'RE PARTICULARLY WILD ABOUT COWBOYS

DESCRIBE YOUR IDEAL MAN (Age, Occupation, Character, etc.) SOMEONE VERY ROMANTIC, ABOUT 35, + WHO LOVES TO TRAVEL. ALSO, WHO HAS A FUNNY PERSONALITY.

DESCRIBE YOUR IDEAL EVENING COCKTAILS, ROMANTIC DINNER, + SLOW DANCING.

DESCRIBE YOURSELF (What kind of person are you?) I AM A VERY KIND-HEARTED PERSON WHO IS FUN TO BE AROUND, BUT CAN BE A SERIOUS PERSON WHEN I NEED TO BE.

IF YOU COULD CHANGE ONE CHARACTER TRAIT IN YOURSELF, IT WOULD BE I'M TOO KIND-HEARTED AT TIMES WHY? BECAUSE PEOPLE TAKE ADVANTAGE OF ME.

AMBITIONS (What you want from life in general) TO STAY SINGLE + JUST HAVE FUN FOR A WHILE — LATER I'LL GET MARRIED + HOPEFULLY HAVE A DAUGHTER

WHY DO YOU WANT TO BE A PLAYMATE? IT'S JUST BEEN ONE OF MY DREAMS! I'VE ALWAYS WONDERED IF I COULD BE A PLAYMATE + HOW I WOULD FEEL!

DESCRIBE THE CIRCUMSTANCES THAT LED TO YOUR APPLYING TO BE A PLAYMATE I'VE ALWAYS TRIED LOOKING IN THE MAGAZINES TO FIND AN ADDRESS, BUT COULDN'T. I SAW ERIC REDDING'S AD IN THE NEWSPAPER FROM YOU GUYS.

DID YOU SEND THE PICTURES IN YOURSELF? NO

DID A PHOTOGRAPHER OR TALENT SCOUT APPROACH YOU? ERIC REDDING

OTHER UNUSUAL BIOGRAPHICAL INFORMATION AT 5'11", I TOWER OVER A LOT OF MY DATES, AND HAVE TO LAUGH ABOUT IT SOMETIMES.

ADDITIONAL COMMENTS I WOULD LOVE TO BE A PLAYMATE, AND IF I DO, ONE OF MY DREAMS WOULD HAVE COME TRUE!

MODEL RELEASE

To Playboy Enterprises, Inc. ("PLAYBOY"), 680 North Lake Shore Drive, Chicago, Illinois 60611: In consideration of my being considered as a candidate for the PLAYBOY Magazine "Playmate of the Month" and for other good and valuable consideration, receipt of which I acknowledge, and with knowledge that you intend to act in reliance hereon I irrevocably give you, your subsidiaries, affiliates, agents, successors, assigns and licensees all right, title and interest, including all copyright and other literary property, commercial and publication rights in and to, and the absolute right and permission to copyright, use, publish and distribute in whole or in part, all photographs (whether made as stills, motion pictures or on video tape) in which I may be included, and my name (whether real or fictitious), my voice and any biographical material pertaining to me, for editorial, advertising, art or promotion, or for any lawful purpose whatsoever in any and all media in perpetuity worldwide and without restrictions. I am posing for the photographs as an independent contractor and not as an employee, and I release you from the responsibility of unemployment reporting and other employment associated duties.

I hereby waive any right to inspect or object to the finished product and the printed material that may be used in conjunction therewith and the use to which it may be applied.

I hereby certify that I have not posed for any nude or semi-nude photographs except those now being submitted to PLAYBOY, with exceptions as noted. (The term "semi-nude" is defined as any pose in attire more revealing than that usually seen on a public beach in the United States.) I further certify that I have not been guilty of any illegal action (Other than such things as minor traffic offenses) which might damage the PLAYBOY image or lessen my promotional value to PLAYBOY.

I further agree that I will do no posing in the nude or semi-nude for still photography,motion pictures, or for any commercial purposes whatsoever (such as night clubs) until you advise me whether or not I have been accepted as a Playmate of the Month, and if I am so accepted, until two years after the cover date of the issue in which I appear as Playmate. Exception to this rule can only be made by written permission from PLAYBOY.

I hereby release, discharge and agree to save PLAYBOY harmless from any liability by virtue of any blurring, distortion, alteration, optical illusion or use in composite form, whether intentional or otherwise, that may occur or be produced in taking or reproducing said pictures. I AM 18 YEARS* OF AGE OR OVER OR HAVE HAD THIS FORM SIGNED BY MY PARENT OR GUARDIAN.

Signed _Vickie Smith_ Date _10/2/91_

Permanent State of Residence _TEXAS_

I, as parent or guardian of the minor who signed the above release, consent to the signing of such release, and agree to defend and hold the beneficiaries of the release harmless against any claim that the minor may make (before or after reaching the age of Majority) because of the use of the photographs in any manner permitted by such release. I fully understand that the beneficiaries of the release are and will be relying upon my agreement and signature which are intended to induce them to accept the release.

Signed_____
                        (Parent or Guardian)

Name_____ Date_____
          (Please Print)

Address_____
          No.   Street   City   State   Zip Code

* 19 years in Alabama and 21 years in Mississippi, Nebraska, Pennsylvania and Puerto Rico.

PHOTOGRAPHER'S AGREEMENT

I hereby certify that I am submitting to PLAYBOY all nude or semi-nude photographs, negatives and transparencies that I have already taken of this Playmate candidate. In the event that she is accepted as a Playmate of the Month, I further certify (in consideration for value received, receipt whereof is acknowledged) that I will submit all photographs, negatives and transparencies of her which I must take to fulfill PLAYBOY requirements. I agree that, upon completion of this Playmate shooting, I will not take any further nude or semi-nude photographs of this model, except when specifically assigned to do so by PLAYBOY, for a period of two years from this date or the date when I have completed these shootings, whichever date is later. I certify that I have no knowledge or any reason to believe that this model is guilty of any illegal action (other than such things as minor traffic offenses) which might damage the PLAYBOY image or lessen her promotional value to PLAYBOY. I further agree that all nude or semi-nude photographs I have taken of this model shall become the sole property of PLAYBOY. (The term "semi-nude" is defined as any pose in attire more revealing than that usually seen on a public beach in the United States.) In the event PLAYBOY elects to photograph, on motion picture film, video tape or otherwise, one or more photographic sessions with this Playmate candidate, and in the event I am included in said photography as a subject, I hereby grant to PLAYBOY the right to use said photography of me, plus my name, voice and biographical material, for any lawful purpose whatsoever in any and all media in perpetuity worldwide and without restrictions.

Photographer _Eric Redd_ Date _10/2/91_

Witness_____

ANY ALTERATION OR ADDITION TO THIS RELEASE IS NOT VALID UNLESS ACCEPTED IN WRITING BY PLAYBOY ENTERPRISES,INC.

Chapter 5

We don't know if a record was set, but only three days after the film on Vickie arrived in the Los Angeles offices of *Playboy*, Linda Kenney called Eric. She wanted to speak to Vickie and then have her get out to Los Angeles as soon as it could be arranged.

It's always great to be the bearers of great news, and we wanted to deliver this in person to Vickie. Eric called and asked her to get over to the studio. Normally it took her about an hour to drive in from her apartment, but this time she made it in thirty minutes. When she walked in the door, it was clear she had figured out something good was going on. Her smile lit up the room like a strobe.

"Guess what, darlin'," Eric said. "You're going to be a *Playboy* Playmate!"

The three of us hugged and laughed, then hugged again. It truly was a moment we would never forget. The sheer *promise* of it all was so palpable! When Vickie managed to regain her composure, Eric told her that she needed to talk to Linda and photo coordinator Stephanie Barnett. They would arrange for her to fly out the next weekend. Once there, they would talk to her, and she would be photographed some more.

We left Vickie alone for the twenty minutes she was on the phone with Linda Kenney and don't have any firsthand knowledge of what transpired. We do know that after Vickie hung up, she appeared confused and somewhat angry. Eric was naturally concerned. This was Big Break Time, Dream Come True Time, what could be bothering her?

"I'm mad at you," she said.

"Why?"

"I thought you told me they were going to fly me to Los Angeles."

"They are," Eric said, growing more bewildered by the moment.

Vickie shook her head. "No, they're not. They said they're flying me to *California!*"

Eric just stood there for a minute with his mouth open. It was such a bizarre statement that he fully expected her to burst out laughing and tell him she was kidding. But no, she was serious.

It took a while before Eric was able to make her believe that Los Angeles was in California. Even with D'eva's help, Vickie thought he was trying to pull a fast one. She was under the almost unshakeable impression that Los Angeles was in New York. Finally Vickie got her coasts straightened out. American students have been shown to have a dismal knowledge of geography, but this wasn't Liechtenstein we were talking about.

The incident was more than a little unsettling. We knew from her difficulty in filling out a simple one-page biography that we weren't dealing with a candidate for a Nobel Prize in anything. Still, this was a bit much and more than a bit worrisome. Was this a case of a deficiency in the American educational system or a deficiency in her brain capacity? In either case, it was clear this girl needed management. Brighter, savvier women had crashed in the fast lanes of Los Angeles. Since we were the ones sending her there, we volunteered to help her navigate.

Getting ready for the trip to L.A. proved to be an adventure in itself. We told Vickie that if she had any questions or problems, she should call us any time, day or night. She really had no idea what to do. This twenty-four-year-old girl/woman had yet to venture out of her home state (or at least that's what she told us), and from what we could ascertain, had done very little venturing within her home state. Now she was going to the Playboy mansion. It was heady, and exciting, and terrifying for her.

Vickie called every one of the next six days as she prepared for her adventure. Sometimes four or five times a day. Who else could she turn to? Virgie? Aunt Kay? They were less-seasoned travelers than she was.

Even luggage was a big issue. For starters, she had none and didn't want to borrow any. It wasn't until the day before her departure—no, the night before—that she went somewhere and bought three pieces of matching luggage. She was thrilled with them. It seemed as if those suitcases represented her bright new future: money, fame, success. And they were matching.

Her unsophisticated enthusiasm and nervous exhilaration was understandable. The kid had grown up with nothing. And suddenly she was invited into a world that represented the epitome of glamor to her, the world of Hugh Hefner and Playboy bunnies. It was the stuff her dreams were made of, and she had just been handed a first-class ticket. Actually, Playboy booked her in coach, but hey, Vickie was revved so high, she could have flown to L.A. on her own power.

Vickie's difficulty in getting her luggage act together was one of our smaller concerns. Some of her other worries had us worried. For instance there was the call the night before she was to leave. It was late, and we hadn't heard from Vickie all day. That in itself had us wondering since she'd been calling so often. But we dismissed it, figuring she was busy shopping and getting ready.

When she did call, she told Eric something had been bothering her all day. It was a rumor she'd heard. Was it really true that to even be considered for a centerfold, a girl had to sleep with Mr. Hefner?

With someone else, Eric might have joked about the silliness of the rumor, but Vickie was clearly upset and taking it seriously. Instead Eric said, "I honestly don't know firsthand, but since Mr. Hefner is married now and just had a child, I kind of doubt it." He went on to assure her that the people of Playboy select the Playmates with great care and professionalism, and she really didn't have to worry about sleeping with Hugh Hefner.

She seemed satisfied with that response and said goodbye. She promised that her next call would be from the Playboy mansion.

About five minutes later, the phone rang again. It was Vickie.

"I have one more question," she said. "Do you have a minute?"

"Sure, what is it?" Eric asked.

"Well, uh, do you know if the girls have to run around naked the whole time they stay at the mansion, or when they're working at the studio?"

This time Eric had to laugh. "No, honey," he said. "These are all professional people. They'll treat you like a lady. I promise."

Her sigh came across the wires, and Eric could feel her relief. Who had been filling her head with this nonsense?

She said goodbye and hung up. Eric hadn't made it to the next room when the phone rang still another time.

"This is the last time I'll bother you guys, but I just remembered something."

"Yes?"

"They said that they're going to pick me up at the airport in a black-and-white limousine. I was wondering what they mean exactly. Do they mean a black-and-white checkered one like you find on the floors in restaurants, or what?"

Eric had to sit down. This was going from mildly amusing to seriously bizarre. Yet he knew she was earnestly confused. He explained that it would be either a white limo with a black console top, or a black limo with a white top. But she didn't have to worry—the driver would have a sign with her name on it. All she had to do was find the driver.

She thanked him again. Actually, it was pretty sweet, and they said their goodbyes—this time for real.

Vickie first checked in with us Monday night from the guest quarters of the Playboy Mansion. She'd arrived safely, but she did have a bit of trouble at the airport. She'd been surprised at how much luggage was at baggage claim and how much alike the suitcases were. It took her a long time to find hers, but when she did, the nice driver had carried them to the limousine (which, by the way, was black with a white console top).

She hadn't been in the mansion for more than thirty minutes when a phone call came from the airline. She had walked off with the wrong luggage, and what she had taken didn't even remotely resemble the set she had so lovingly and proudly chosen.

The nice driver had to return to the airport to make the switch. Vickie apologized to him, explaining, "Well, they all looked alike to me." What was never explained was how the airlines found Vickie at the Playboy mansion.

*T*he next day, Linda Kenney reached Eric. He could tell things were working out well by the tone in her voice. She'd always been professional and courteous to him, but that afternoon she sounded giddy with enthusiasm. She wanted to tell him that she and West Coast photo editor Marilyn Grabowski were in love with Vickie, and that she was one of the best models to come along in ages. They just wanted to congratulate us on finding Vickie and having such good instincts about her.

We were thrilled that it was all turning out so well, and then came the topper—Marilyn had already decided to feature Vickie on the cover of the March 1992 issue of *Playboy!*

Playboy is in the business of selling magazines, and the staff there often go with their gut feelings on what the public wants to see. As far they were concerned, a voluptuous blonde beauty by the name of Vickie Lynn Smith was what the public was waiting for.

Chapter 6

*T*he news out of Los Angeles had been great, and we figured it was clear sailing for Vickie from then on. What we hadn't figured, however, was that LaLa Land got a bit LaLa-ier with her arrival.

Eric got the distress call. Vickie sounded more upset than usual. Before she could launch into what was bothering her, Eric interrupted. If what she had to say was confidential, she might want to find a pay phone somewhere. He had been told phone conversations from the guest quarters at the mansion were recorded. Vickie was silent for a moment and then she said she'd get back to him.

Eric made up a hundred scenarios while he was waiting. Things had been going so well that he couldn't imagine what had caused that alarm in Vickie's voice. Had he steered her wrong—*was* she really expected to sleep with Hefner? It seemed inconceivable, but what else could it be?

Finally, an hour later, Vickie got back to him. She had found a public phone, although Eric wasn't sure how or where.

"Eric." Vickie's voice was shaking. "Are there cameras in the guest rooms?"

"Cameras?"

"You know, security cameras."

He had no idea, of course, but Vickie seemed desperate to know, so he promised to find out what he could. His next question was why she cared. She answered, "Please, just find out and I'll tell you later."

Eric contacted Linda Kenney. Apparently this was not a question that arose very often, and she didn't have the answer but promised to check into it.

It didn't take Linda long to get back to Eric. She had discovered that, yes, there were video cameras installed behind the air-conditioning vents in the guest rooms. For security purposes only, she said. Linda showed remarkable restraint and tact. She didn't ask why he needed to know about the cameras. Of course, Eric didn't know himself.

That evening, a panicky Vickie got through from a pay phone at the Playboy studios. Did Eric know? Were there cameras? When Eric confirmed that there were, she gasped and then was silent. After waiting a long time, it felt like several minutes, Eric asked her what was going on.

It seems Vickie had packed some toys in her matching set of luggage to keep her amused. Sex toys. To help her wile away those long, lonely hours at night.

"You mean you masturbated?" Eric asked. " Well, that's no big deal. I'm sure they couldn't see anything with the lights off."

"No," she said. "You don't understand. The lights were on. I was, um, at the mirror."

"What?"

"I was there for, like maybe two hours," she said, near tears. "All the lights were on and everything. Eric, I used all my stuff."

"Stuff?"

"You know, like um, dildos and shit."

"I see," he said, even though he was having trouble assimilating what she was telling him.

This "show" had evidently gone on every night for six nights. She hadn't thought a thing about it—it was her way of relieving stress—until one of the other girls mentioned the cameras.

Eric tried his best to calm her. Of all the places she could have indulged in this pastime, the Playboy mansion was probably the safest. It didn't matter what he said, she was inconsolable and worried that this peccadillo would ruin her brand-new career. Of course, Eric had no way of knowing then that Vickie wasn't a stranger to masturbating for an audience. It was something she used to do at the topless clubs.

First thing the next morning, Eric was on the phone to Linda Kenney. Hearing the rundown of Vickie's confession, Linda became hysterical—laughing. She could barely breathe and kept repeating, "You're kidding!" Each time Eric assured her he wasn't, she went off again.

Finally, when Linda could speak with a reasonable amount of control, she told him not to worry. The mansion staff was incredibly discreet, and no one would blow the whistle on Vickie.

Later Eric found out that the security crew at the mansion all got copies of the surveillance camera tapes. They're undoubtedly collector's items now.

*T*here were no repercussions from the security camera escapade. If anything *Playboy* loved Vickie. That same magic that had been evident in the PMT was alive and well in California. The pictures were stupendous, and Marilyn Grabowski told Vickie, Linda, and many others that Vickie was the most beautiful woman she'd ever seen, even without makeup.

Ironically, the March 1992 cover they chose for Vickie's debut had a debutante theme. They dressed her in an emerald green gown, seated her on an ornate antique chair, and somehow made her look like a lush, full-figured Grace Kelly. This poor kid from nowhere, with no education, and no sophistication was chosen as a symbol of old-world money, class and elegance. It was probably an inside joke on *Playboy*'s part, but if anyone ever burned with the desire to be a sparkly deb, it was Vickie Lynn Smith.

*I*t was about this time that Vickie's past rose up and bit her in the rear. The staff had examined her biography and noticed the word dancer had been scratched out and replaced by the word model. Stephanie called the number Vickie had provided and reached Gigi's Cabaret.

Playboy is an American institution. It sends out scouts to Ivy League campuses in search of Playmates. It courts schoolteachers and police officers. It will accept girls who work in upscale places like Rick's. It definitely does not want strippers, especially not ones who table-dance at Gigi's Cabaret.

When Linda Kenney came straight out and asked Eric if Vickie had been a stripper, he covered for her. He told Linda he didn't think so. He barely knew Vickie and although she had said she was a dancer, he wasn't sure at that point if it had been nude dancing or just topless dancing. Again, *Playboy* drew a line at baring of breasts and baring it all. David Davari, the owner of Gigi's at that time was also called, and he, too, covered for Vickie.

Vickie told Linda Kenney and Marilyn Grabowski that she had been a dancer for a very short time, only because she'd been forced into it to support her son.

For a while it seemed that *Playboy* was going to back away from Vickie. She wasn't coming across as its archetypical fresh and unspoiled girl next door. But instead of giving her a ticket back to Houston, Vickie was given a centerfold.

A cover pays $500, a centerfold a nice $20,000 plus promotional gigs that can really add up. Vickie was going to be Miss May 1992, bumping several other girls to later issues.

Ordinarily a model doesn't make the centerfold so quickly, but Vickie was strapped for money. Payment to the models is due upon publication, and Vickie didn't want to wait. The fact that *Playboy* was willing to accommodate her was a testament to how much she was liked there. When Vickie was named Playmate of the Year, she received another $100,000 and a Jaguar. All in all, it sure beat dancing at Gigi's—if you didn't count potential income from octogenarians who wandered in for lunch.

Chapter 7

Vickie's cover shot for March 1992 hit the newsstands at the end of January, transforming her into a minor Houston celebrity. One of the first fringe benefits to her new fame was a gorgeous firefighter named Al Bolt.

Al met Vickie in January at the Silverado Club, a country and western place outside of Houston. Every year as a fund-raiser to benefit burned and crippled children, the Houston Fire Department issues a calendar featuring its best-looking guys. Al was one of them. He was at the Silverado signing the calendar, and Vickie was autographing her *Playboy* cover. We knew Al from photographing the calendar, so we introduced him to Vickie.

Al, a divorcee with three children, said, "I was attracted to her by the way she was being presented as a home-town girl from right here in Texas. Came up dirt poor, made it big, decided she was going to try out for the *Playboy* centerfold, and like within three days, they called her back and said, yes, you're the one we want."

As part of the fund-raising, the firemen were auctioned off for dances. Vickie was not happy when her mother Virgie won him with a $75 bid. Later, she gave Al an autographed cover of *Playboy* on which she had written "To Al, I would have paid a whole lot more."

That was more than enough encouragement for Al. He didn't just give Vickie his phone number. He gave her his pager number, his office number, and his car phone number as well. However, Vickie didn't call them. It wasn't that she hadn't been attracted to the handsome, dark-haired fireman/paramedic, it was just that *Playboy* commitments were gobbling up her time.

She was somewhere nearly every night, signing photographs and layouts, hosting talent searches for *Playboy*, going to parties, spending her money. There were the trips to the Playboy mansion.

So it must have been kismet when Al, on an excursion with his kids at a park in Tomball, saw Virgie assisting some traffic accident victims. After things settled down, Al reintroduced himself to Virgie and asked her for Vickie's phone number.

Virgie obliged. When Al reached Vickie, he explained how he got her number and she indicated she didn't mind.

Their first date was in March 1992. It was casual, lunch, no pressure. Al brought along her centerfold, which Vickie auto-graphed with a smiling heart above her name. Al was charmed at how shy she was, how innocent and sweet.

That isn't to say he wasn't knocked out by the lady's physique. And that face. But it was the whole picture that gave Al his mission. He wanted this girl; he wanted to take care of her, to protect her, to make sure she came to no harm.

It was all so clear for him at the beginning.

"It started out as a daytime thing," Al said. "Eventually, we started going to nightclubs like the Yucatan and Bayou Mama's. These weren't dinner dates, though. This was publicity. Being part of the *Playboy* crowd. At that time Vickie was representing *Playboy*, and she wanted me to be there with her. I kind of fell into being her boyfriend."

Put two healthy young people together, and things are bound to heat up. "When Vickie wants to win you over, she could pour on the charm," Al said. "Her idol was Marilyn Monroe, so she would come on with that soft, smooth kind of voice that told you...whatever she wanted, she could use that to lure you into whatever she wanted you to do."

Soon, Al was invited to Vickie's house. Kay Beall, her boyfriend Floyd Harrison, and daughter Melinda were all staying with her at that time. Mostly to watch Daniel. But also to reap some of the rewards of Vickie's new financial status.

Al was surprised by her relatives. "They were really country oriented," he said. "When I say country oriented, I mean there's country people that are poor but clean. Then you have country people that are poor, trashy, and lost. I would say that they were more the poor, trashy, and lost.

"Her Aunt Kay was very large, very sloppy. Vickie invited her to come from Mexia to Houston to watch out for Daniel. So, the whole family just moved in. They were all living there and none of them worked. Vickie was the only breadwinner. Where she was getting her money, I don't know. Because she didn't have a job. She just had the centerfold."

It didn't take long, however, for Al to get an inkling of the source of Vickie's money. "The income was coming from a guy that I found out about after our relationship was going on. His name was Howard Marshall. He was supposed to have been an oil tycoon that lived in River Oaks."

Vickie told Al about meeting Marshall, although in her version, it was in a restaurant. "His driver had come over and asked her to go and talk to him. Vickie told me that she 'brought him back from the dead.' She told me he was really down because his wife had died. That he didn't have anybody to talk to and all that kind of stuff. So she went over and talked to him, and that's how they became good friends."

Of course, it wasn't just Marshall's wife who had passed away, but also Lady Walker, his mistress. And not many customers went to Gigi's for the food. And, of course, there was more to Vickie and Marshall's relationship than idle chit chat.

But Al didn't know any of that. He still saw Vickie as the sweet young thing from Mexia. Slowly, the truth started to come to light.

Visits with Vickie's relatives disabused him of any thoughts she was getting money from them. "They had no money. Nothing. [Their house] had bugs crawling on the furniture and things like that. It wasn't very clean."

Then he found the pay stub in Vickie's car. It was from J. Howard Marshall's company. "She went into a store one time and I happened to be driving her car. And on the side of the door, there's like this pocket thing. There was a check stub sticking up out of it. I picked it up. It had Howard Marshall's name on the top of it and his company. Down below it had Vickie's name as the recipient. So, I felt like maybe he was carrying her as an employee and just paying her, but she didn't do anything for him. At least not for the company."

Al began to suspect that Marshall was paying Vickie for sexual favors.

"She had a brand new Toyota Celica, I remember. White. And she got that before she did the *Playboy* layout. The money didn't come from her family. It all came from Howard Marshall. I heard later that the old man liked to watch. That he would like it when Vickie was with another girl. He'd pay 'em to watch the sex act. He was too old to do much for himself, but I know Vickie serviced him."

Then there was the matter of the phone calls. Al's relationship with Vickie only lasted nine months, but for a brief time, they lived together. "I might be in the bed laying right beside her, and we might be laughing and cutting up and having a good time. All of a sudden the phone would ring. When she'd pick it up, she'd put her finger to her mouth and tell me to be quiet because it was Howard. She'd cover the phone and tell me to hush.

"She didn't want him to know that I was in her life. Howard was not to know about me at all. She felt like if he knew about me, her days of money would be over with...It would upset me. We would have arguments about it. I would tell her, hey...I'm a person, too. I'm a human being, too. I don't have a lot of money, but the problem is, you say he's a businessman, well, I'm a businessman, too."

That argument didn't carry much weight with Vickie. According to Al, she was at Marshall's beck and call. If he wanted a platter of sandwiches, she would race out and get it for him. What Al resented was Vickie would elicit his help as well. "It kind of made me sick...I'm supposed to be her boyfriend, yet she's going with this old, antique rascal that I guess was her sugar daddy. He'd given her a tennis bracelet that had multiple diamonds on it. He'd given her rings. Diamond earrings. I'm talking real big diamonds.

A person on a fire department salary would never be able to maintain the lifestyle that she was hunting for."

As Al's relationship with Vickie continued, more and more of her wildness surfaced. Once when they were driving back from Mexia, Vickie decided it would be fun to flash truckers on the highway. She opened the car's moonroof, and when the car pulled close to a truck, she'd expose her breasts. "Those truckers would blow their horns and stuff," Al said. "She'd say 'Now speed up and get to the next one.' Well, you know that they've got CB radios. All of them knew she was coming. She flashed every truck from Mexia to Houston."

Al hung in, even though friends were cluing him in on Vickie's past. He wasn't sure if they were jealous that he was dating her or were genuinely concerned for him. "What they didn't know was that I was trying to change her from the inside. Being that I'm a Christian, I took that as a challenge. I was looking at a soul that was out of control and that maybe...I could get her to turn around."

Al had no idea what kind of challenge he had taken on.

Chapter 8

*B*ecoming a *Playboy* centerfold meant Vickie could leave her dancing days behind her, along with many of her friends who were told that *Playboy* didn't want her to associate with them anymore. Vickie represented the magazine now. She would continue to bare her body but with a degree of respectability that the titty bars could never attain. When it's for two hundred bucks a night on a dark stage, it's dirty and sneered at. When it's for twenty thousand bucks in a national magazine—it's admired and applauded.

We had signed on as Vickie's managers, and a large part of that task turned out to be baby-sitting. Vickie was a wild girl, and as we got to know her better, we discovered that her taste for the fun life was quite catholic.

She liked partying, any kind, all kind. Sex, any sex. Drugs and alcohol, as long as it was in excess. It was a struggle keeping her sober enough for promotional events. Sobriety wasn't the only problem. There was her diet, her appearance, her propensity for picking up men or women or men *and* women for the night.

Whenever possible, we went with Vickie to her publicity events, and when that wasn't an option, we tried to line up chaperons.

We weren't always successful keeping her under rein.

In February 1992, Houston hosted the annual Livestock Show and Rodeo. Joe Healy, director of marketing and advertising for the Appletree Grocery Store chain, hired Vickie to represent his company. She was to ride on a float, along with Ray Childress, all-pro defensive linebacker for the NFL's Houston Oilers.

Childress made it clear he wasn't happy having to associate with Vickie, even to the limited extent of sitting next to her on the float. But she behaved well enough that Childress was able to remain civil.

As if turned out, Vickie was interested in him for more than his number of sacks on the field. It made no difference to her that he was married. She asked Eric if he thought Childress had a big "package." She'd noticed his large hands and to her that meant only one thing. She asked the linebacker if he wanted to take her dancing, but he, wisely, declined.

Later that week, Vickie's job was to mingle with clients in the skyboxes, shake a few hands, and act the gracious hostess. Apparently the open bar was too much of a temptation for her. It didn't take long before she was drunk, boisterous, and something far from gracious.

According to Deborah Keener, account executive for country

radio station 92.9, the main topic of conversation that night was not the rodeo, but Vickie Lynn Smith. Seems they were expecting a more typical *Playboy* bunny—slim, attractive, classy. What they got was Vickie—big, inebriated, coarse.

Still, Joe Healy used her again later that year. In conjunction with East Texas Distributing, he hired her as the celebrity spokesperson for their booth at a New Orleans convention.

Two days before the event, Vickie let Eric know she was unhappy with the deal: five hundred a day for two days. Although she'd agreed to the fee because of the free time she'd have in New Orleans—it would be something of a paid vacation—she informed Eric that she wouldn't go unless she got more money. Her new rate was now two thousand a day for all public appearances.

Eric tried to reason with her, pointing out the contract had been on the books for seven or eight months. It fell on deaf ears and limited scruples. She wouldn't get on the plane unless her demands were met.

Eric called Ken Stilling, vice-president for East Texas Distributing, and told him the situation. Ken, ever the gentleman, offered to renegotiate the deal directly with Vickie. After all, his invitations had been sent out. He had his own reputation to consider.

Ken never told Eric the details of the agreement he and Vickie reached, but it was clear he bent to her money demands. However, her tantrum created a great deal of embarrassment and a professional rift between us and East Texas Distributing. More than that, it signaled the beginning of the end for the management relationship between Vickie and Britt Redding Associates.

The actual New Orleans event went well; Vickie signed autographs and did a standout job. It was after hours that things went to hell.

*V*ickie had brought along a friend. Missy was the name she gave, but later Joe found out her real name was Melissa Byrum. Vickie had met Missy at a car show promotion in Ohio that spring. Vickie also brought her son, Daniel, who was six at the time.

"Working with Vickie at the convention was one of utter disbelief and disgust," Joe told Eric. "Vickie worked very well with the people all day at the booth signing autographs, mingling, you know. Things began to unravel at the end of the day when Vickie started to get bored. She wanted to start drinking."

Vickie became intoxicated but still managed to persuade Missy, Ken Stilling, and Joe to hit Bourbon Street. Even poor little Daniel was to be included in the party.

Joe hesitated, wondering if it wasn't better to leave the boy behind, but Vickie was adamant. She wouldn't leave Daniel by himself in the hotel. Besides, she said, Daniel was "used to hanging out with his mom."

Again, Joe and Ken tried to discourage her, but Vickie refused to budge. Missy couldn't have cared less either way—she just wanted to party.

Daniel may have been accustomed to accompanying his mother, but that didn't mean he liked it. He started to cry in protest. Vickie told him to hush, and the little boy was forced to go along.

Bourbon Street. It has bars, jazz clubs, stunning Spanish and French architecture, and of course, the world-class cuisine. And it's also known for its wild side—the porno shops, hookers of both sexes, muggers who prey on tourists.

It was clear immediately that Vickie wanted to concentrate on one aspect of that infamous district: the bars.

The group went from one to another. Joe and Ken attempted to keep things under control, but as the night progressed, and

Vickie got more and more inebriated, they recognized that there was no stopping this girl.

The drunker she got, the wilder she got—at one point she declared loud enough to be heard in Biloxi that she didn't need to wear a top anymore. And, in front of her son, Daniel, and her bosses, Joe Healy and Ken Stilling, she whipped off her blouse to reveal Dr. Johnson's efforts in pyramid building. Naturally, there was no bra.

Vickie bounced to the center of the street, where she could show off to the most people. Of course, the tourists and the locals went wild. According to Joe, Vickie nearly started a riot. Soon, onlookers wanted more, and Vickie didn't object. Strangers fondled her, both men and women. Mind you, Daniel was there, witnessing the entire bacchanal.

Eventually, the novelty of her impromptu titty dance wore thin, and Joe was hopeful that the horror of an evening was over. But no, there was still room left on Vickie's dance card.

Vickie spotted an adult toy store. She grabbed Missy's hand and led her inside. Between the two of them, they spent more than five hundred dollars on the specialty merchandise. Dildos of all kind: strap on, double-headed, electric. Then there were the vibrators, lotions, masks, cuffs, and more. Daniel observed it all.

At this point, Joe and Ken had had enough. Daniel was clearly overtired and overstimulated, and the adults were drunk. They were able to persuade Vickie to head back to the hotel.

"You won't believe what happened next," Joe told Eric. "Once we were in the elevator, Vickie and Missy started ripping each other's clothes off. In the damn *elevator*. In front of Ken and me and Daniel, for God's sake. They started kissing each other and groping each other." Joe paused, the very memory made his neck flush red.

"Vickie and Missy then pulled out some of the sex toys that they had just bought and started to carry on with those...like inserting them in each other."

When the elevator reached their floor, he and Ken bailed out. Neither one had ever seen anything like it. It was as if Vickie was from another world, a place where morals, standards, and propriety had no meaning.

The next morning, actually later that morning, the whole group came together again for brunch. Nothing was said about the events of the night before. Vickie acted as if she didn't have a care in the world, except for the hangover, of course. Missy stayed quiet. Daniel wanted pancakes. Joe and Ken wanted to get the conference over with, deposit Vickie on the plane, and return to a semblance of sanity. Mostly, though, they thought about Daniel and the effect his mother's behavior was having on such a young psyche.

Vickie had no such worries. When asked about the situation, she would say, "If I treat Daniel like an adult and keep him around in adult situations, he will mature quicker." Somehow, we never thought she got that from Dr. Spock.

Her attitude toward Daniel's education had shocked more than Joe and Ken. Al Bolt remembers many evenings when he, Vickie, and little Daniel would watch videos—Vickie's *Playboy* videos.

"Her son was right there in the room," he said. "I would talk to her. Tell her it wasn't good for Daniel to see her all naked and sexy." She countered that Daniel knew what she did for a living and that she wasn't ashamed of anything.

Chapter 9

$\mathcal{B}$ack home in Texas, things were deteriorating between Vickie and Al Bolt. They'd been together since January 1992, and in March he moved into her house. At the time, Vickie's Aunt Kay Beall, boyfriend Floyd Harrison, and her niece Melinda were all living in the house, too. However, once Al settled himself in, the family moved back to Mexia.

Vickie still continued to meet Howard Marshall often, usually at the River Oaks Country Club.

Al's position as man of the house mostly consisted of doing the housecleaning and laundry. He tried hard to be a good role model for Daniel, but it wasn't easy. The place was a mess, and the more Al tried to make it liveable, the less Vickie seemed to like him. Finally, she hired a maid—Maria Cerrato. Whatever she wanted from Al didn't include a feather duster and Windex.

Her drinking and drug taking were reaching new heights—or depths, depending on your perspective. Al told of a time when Vickie took him out to Mexia, and they stayed at the Drillin' Rig motel.

Vickie invited an old school friend, Tim, to the room for drinks. Lots of drinks, as it turned out. Eventually Tim staggered off, and Al put Vickie to bed. This wasn't the first time Al had to take care of her when she was beyond walking under her own power. "I would physically carry her to the bathroom. Then I would take her and put her in bed. It would get to the point where she would actually urinate in the bed."

"I would go to sleep and miss taking her to the bathroom, and she would just let it go in the bed. I don't think she really realized how much help I was trying to give her. She felt like I was trying to run her life. I wasn't. I was trying to help her get on a good track. There were times when we were at her house, she would talk about her old boyfriends. About how they weren't good for her or just wanted her money. Then she'd say that I was better for Daniel. A father figure."

But it was no use. Their fights became more frequent. And Al was never able to accept her relationship with Marshall. In August, they split up.

Vickie let go a lot quicker than Al. Even though he finally knew the truth about Vickie—that she wasn't the sweet young thing of her press kit but an ex-topless dancer with extracurricular tricks for adding to her income and a current mistress—he had fallen in love with her. He wanted to save her.

The only problem was Vickie had no desire to be saved.

The most devastating aspect of their relationship happened at the end. Al was and is a religious man. He attends church regularly and volunteers his time to charitable causes. His three children mean the world to him, so when he discovered Vickie was pregnant with his child, he naturally wanted to marry Vickie.

"Vickie and I would have had a beautiful kid together," he told Eric. "She was dying to have a baby girl. At least that's what she said. She had that hope chest in her bedroom. The one with dolls and girls clothes."

It was not to be. There would be no marriage and no child. At first Vickie told Al that she wasn't pregnant. However, she did confide to us that she was, indeed, carrying Al's child.

Then Vickie dropped a bombshell on Al. They were arguing again. It was the very end of the relationship, and things had grown bitter. But nothing could have prepared Al for the news Vickie gave him—in public. She told him, with bystanders taking in what could have been a scene on *The Young and the Restless*, that she had been pregnant with his child, but it was just too damn bad. She'd aborted the baby, and she was through with him.

Al was crushed. Abortion was against everything he believed in. He had truly loved Vickie and had wanted another child. How could she have made that decision without consulting him?

After it was over, Al continued to call Vickie. Often enough for Vickie to start proceedings on a restraining order. Her attorney, Saul Gower, warned the fireman to keep his distance, and, with the threat of being arrested, Al did.

But he still carries a large wound. Even now, he can't talk about Vickie without getting upset, without wishing he'd done things differently, without shaking his head about Daniel.

As for Vickie? She was off and running.

By the time she and Al said goodbye for the last time, she had already made another *Playboy* video. She took the cameras to Mexia, where she pouted her way through a tour of her old haunts. There was a new man in her life—bodybuilder Alan Mielsch. Only thing wrong with that relationship was that Alan was married with two children at the time. But the affair only lasted a few months.

Vickie went on promotional tours and signed thousands of autographs. This wasn't easy for her. Spelling was not something she'd mastered—Fred could be spelled Fread, Andrew could be Andru.

We accompanied her to most of these sessions, having worked out a system. If Vickie needed assistance spelling someone's name, she gave us one look. If she needed help writing the personalized message, she had another signal, and there was a third one if the person asking for her autograph frightened her or bothered her.

However, despite the worrisome spelling and occasional creep, Vickie was in heaven. Nothing pleased her more than being center stage. The centerfold put her there. She was a celebrity. Men wanted her. Women wanted her. Vickie had no intention of letting them down.

A typical night would include an appearance in at least one nightclub. Not necessarily to work, but definitely to be seen. Alcohol eased the way, softened the edges, turned her on.

One night, she'd gone to dinner with us and a lovely young blonde named Colleen Rafferty. Several bottles of champagne later, we left the Palm restaurant and went to a karaoke bar called The Sing-A-Long Club.

Of course, Vickie needed to be drunk to get up on the stage and alternated between beer and champagne. After an hour of steady consumption, she went to the stage to sing and took Colleen with her.

The remarkable thing about this was that Vickie and Colleen had decided earlier that day to dress in identical outfits. Pink-and-white-striped midriff tops and matching shorts. But they looked as much like twins as Danny DeVito and Arnold Schwarzenegger what with Vickie almost six feet tall and weighing about one hundred sixty-five pounds, and Colleen at five foot four in her highest heels and no more than one hundred ten.

Yet there they were, drunk and dressed like demented candy stripers, and neither one of them able to carry a tune. Of course, the song Vickie selected may have been the problem. She'd chosen "My Ding-A-Ling."

The ladies could barely stand, let alone sing. They did have a good time hugging and touching each other. The patrons in the bar hooted and clapped. It was a show they wouldn't soon forget. Mercifully, the song ended and somehow Vickie and Colleen made it back to the table.

It was after midnight, so the night was still young. Vickie decided to take Colleen to the back of the club where they had a photo booth, the kind that spits out four black-and-white shots in sixty seconds. Their laughter nearly drowned out the cowboy singing on stage.

Eric took the opportunity to call Clay Spires, who was back in Vickie's life as her boyfriend of record, and Colleen's boyfriend Jim, asking them to come for the inebriated pair. Which they did, but instead of taking the women home to sleep it off, as Eric had intended, Clay and Jim ordered up another round of drinks.

Just before we were about to leave, Vickie and Colleen went to the restroom. It took so long that Eric got worried. He figured one or both of them was sick, given all they'd had to drink. He went into the hallway leading to the restrooms but discovered sickness was not the source of the delay.

Vickie had Colleen's shirt pulled down to her waist and was kissing her breasts. Neither seemed to mind Eric's intrusion. At one point, Vickie made eye contact with him, and it was very clear that the "audience" made the moment all the sweeter.

We left. After all, it was nothing more than another typical night with Vickie Lynn Smith. Just like the *Playboy* Playmate model search held at Bayou Mama's, a local Houston nightclub.

We hosted the ten-week event. Each girl who wanted to compete was interviewed and had the rules explained, including, of course, the understanding that nudity was involved. Each girl would have nude Polaroids taken of herself before she could compete in the finals.

Twenty-five women made it to the finals. Vickie was a judge, and it was her job to give the winner a trophy and a diamond bunny necklace in addition to the traditional roses.

Vickie had no real say about the winners—none of the judges did. The winner had been determined a week earlier, based on the nude Polaroids. The ceremony was for show.

After the contest, the partying began. As usual Vickie drank champagne as if it were Evian. She'd liked one of the girls, Tracy Johnson, and focused on her when the whole group moved to a place called Randy's for dancing.

Tracy didn't reciprocate Vickie's interest and when it came time to leave, Vickie was an unhappy camper. She didn't like it when things didn't go her way. She was hot, and she wanted action.

She wanted D'eva.

In the middle of the club, with most of the contestants close enough to hear, Vickie declared that she was in the mood and graphically expressed what she wished to do to D'eva.

D'eva was embarrassed, as was Eric and everyone within earshot. Eric hustled Vickie out of the club and drove her home. With great difficulty, he managed to put her to bed, alone, where she passed out as soon as her head hit the pillow.

D'eva took the incident in stride. She'd gotten to know Vickie, and so it wasn't too much of a shock. But from then on, she made it a point to avoid being alone with Vickie.

Chapter 10

*I*n August of 1992, Vickie received a phone call that changed the direction of her life. It would offer something that she had dreamed of her entire life—financial security.

Paul Marciano, the president of Guess? and the brother of fashion designer Georges Marciano, had been impressed with Vickie's *Playboy* spread. More than impressed. He wanted to meet this voluptuous woman, who looked nothing like the thin, waif-like models so in vogue at the time. He got in touch with *Playboy*'s West Coast photo editor Marilyn Grabowski and asked her to arrange a meeting at an Italian restaurant in Houston—"Oh, you know the name of it," Vickie told *Texas Monthly*. "It's got two names. Wait—it's called, uh, Something-Something."

Actually, the restaurant was Anthony's, a popular upscale bistro close to downtown. Once there, Marciano, a dapper man with exquisite taste in clothes and a European sensibility, told Vickie about his quest for the new Guess? girl. He was looking to replace Eva Herzigova, a Marilyn Monroe look-alike, who had come after Claudia Schiffer, a Brigitte Bardot look-alike

Vickie had never heard of Guess? jeans. She did all her shopping at Kmart and Wal-Mart. And Guess? Jeans weren't found hanging on the racks in those establishments. It didn't help that Vickie had trouble understanding Marciano's French accent and had to ask him to write the word "guess," which Marciano pronounced Gee-yess.

Guess? may have been an unknown commodity to Vickie but not to the rest of the world. It was a jeans company with an attitude and certainly could be categorized as a phenomenon in the clothing industry. It began with four brothers, the Moroccan-born sons of a rabbi who were raised in the south of France. Maurice was the financial man, Paul advertising, Armand operations and production, and Georges was the designer.

Guess? arrived in the United States in 1981 just as the designer jeans fad was on the way out. As the story goes, Georges took the company's "Marilyn" jeans—faded denim and so supertight that zippers were needed at the ankles—to Bloomingdale's. The buyer didn't care that the Marilyn style was selling faster than hot crepes in Paris and wouldn't order any. Georges was furious but had enough presence of mind to leave fifty pairs on consignment before he left the store in a huff.

Within three hours, all the jeans—with price tags of more than fifty dollars—had been sold and Guess? was on its way to becoming a billion-dollar company.

There were some bumps in the road of success. Employees quit because they couldn't deal with the acrimony in the brothers' less than brotherly dealings with each other. And then there was the little problem with the Nakash brothers, owners of Jordache Enterprises.

The Nakashes bought half interest in Guess? in 1983. This was not a deal made in heaven, and within a year the Marcianos took legal action to rescind it, basically claiming that Jordache was stealing Guess? designs. After more than five years of nasty legal wrangling, a settlement was reached out of court.

During that time, Guess? continued to grow in sales. Credit is given both to Georges's designs and Paul's approach to advertising. People talked about Guess? ads and the models that were used. Besides Schiffer and Herzigova, there were Carrie Otis and Naomi Campbell.

That Vickie was ignorant of the Guess? phenomenon did not seem to bother Paul Marciano that first night. After dinner he took her to the Galleria, the premiere shopping address in Houston, where he bought her Guess? outfits. Her opinion? "Y'all make real nice clothes."

The next day, Vickie was flown in Marciano's private jet to San Antonio, where a Guess? baby clothes layout was being shot. Despite his attention to Vickie, Marciano wasn't very optimistic about her potential as a Guess? model. She was nothing like the sophisticated swans he was used to. This was a girl from the country. Uneducated, naive, inexperienced. But as long as she was there, he decided to take a few photographs.

Marciano sent her off to get her makeup and hair done while he concentrated on the more important business of the baby clothes shoot. His concentration was broken when Vickie emerged from the trailer. Everything stopped.

"I could not believe what I was seeing," Marciano was to say later. "I had never seen such an extraordinary face. The temperature was 100 degrees, and she was still natural in front of the camera. She could have worked all day. She gave me a hundred different looks."

In a story as close to a fairy tale as you can get without a pumpkin, Marciano used the very first test shot as the centerpiece for his new campaign. Many consider the shot of Vickie—lying in a field, chewing a piece of straw, wearing a red-and-white shirt—the most beautiful of her career. Marciano was impressed enough to give her a three-year, multimillion-dollar contract.

Vickie's involvement with Guess? might have played out differently if, at that first meeting, she had told the truth. Marciano had a strict policy that everyone connected with his company have and maintain a spotless image—except for, maybe, him, of course. It was something of an obsession with him. He asked her point blank if she had anything in her past that could hurt the Guess? image.

Vickie smiled. And finished her wine.

*T*hings moved quickly after that. Marciano and Monique Pillard, an Elite modeling agent in New York Vickie had signed with, hammered out a contract. But first, they decided Vickie Lynn Smith had to go. The name, that is.

It was Paul Marciano who came up with the new name. And so it was that Vickie Lynn Smith was laid to rest in August 1992, and Anna Nicole Smith was born. From then on, there was no more Vickie, it would be Anna Nicole and nothing else.

Marciano didn't stop with a new name. Boxes of clothes began arriving at Anna's newly purchased house with instructions to "use what you will and disregard the rest." Anna did just that. Her rejects went to the Salvation Army. After she thanked her benefactor, she promptly asked if he could send some clothes for her Daniel. Of course, he obliged.

The gifts weren't all so mundane. According to Al Bolt, who was still living with Anna, Marciano flew her to his yacht in Mexico for a three-day cruise. On board, he presented her with a pair of onyx-and-diamond earrings, worth about ten thousand dollars. It was the most extravagant gift she'd ever received from an admirer.

Their relationship continued for several months.

Chapter 11

On Christmas Eve 1992, Anna Nicole had a party at her ranch house for friends and family. The million-dollar ranch was paid for by beau-in-abeyance J. Howard Marshall II. Fifteen acres of land, a barn, a workout area for horses, a swimming pool, a house, and guest quarters. Animals wandered freely—cattle, horses, pigs, chickens, sheep, dogs, cats, even peacocks.

The guest list that night consisted almost entirely of family. Virgie, Melinda, Kay, even Anna's brothers and sister. Only a few friends were invited—us, Debbie Hopkins, Anna's longtime pal and hairdresser, Debbie's husband Bill, Anna's then-boyfriend/bodyguard/personal trainer Alan Mielsch, and a few others.

The house had been decorated with care. There was a fourteen-foot white-flocked Christmas tree by the fireplace with gifts stacked all around it. There were tinsel, candles, poinsettias all over the spacious living room, and Anna's family was deeply impressed.

The food was not the run-of-the-mill Christmas party fare unless your family tradition is pimento-cheese-and-tuna-fish sandwiches, with the crusts cut off the white bread. Fritos and bean dip circulated along with the beer and orange soda. There was champagne, but that was hidden away from the family and only doled out to certain friends. Seems Anna was certain her kin would just guzzle the fine wine down.

When everyone had eaten, Anna Nicole brought out a case of Guess? calendars and Guess? notebooks, and asked her family to stand in line to receive them. She autographed each one, reminding her family that from now on, she was Anna Nicole Smith—Vickie Lynn Smith was dead and buried.

Next came presents, and Anna outdid herself. For us and several relatives there were $400 snake-skin boots. For Virgie, a big-screen television. Daniel got a miniature motorcycle, complete with leather riding clothes, helmet, and boots. Alan Mielsch was gifted a full-sized Harley Davidson motorcycle. Anna's maid, Maria Cerrato, was handed the keys to a red Mustang convertible, and Aunt Kay received a Chrysler LaBaron; both cars were adorned with big red bows.

There was much whooping and hollering during the opening of the presents, but right after the last gift had been given, the family took off. Within fifteen minutes, the entire family had gone. Vanished.

Anna didn't seem concerned by this, but it felt to us that the quick departures were about as ungracious as it gets. Some guests didn't even bother to say goodbye. They just took their booty and made tracks.

We stayed, as did Debbie and Bill and two gay friends of Anna's, Tim and Jeff. Elaine and Melvin Tabers lived in the guest quarters, and they retired for the night. Kay and Melinda Beall stayed at the main house, but they went up to bed moments after they'd received their gifts.

Once the relatives were gone, Anna brought out the champagne, vodka, and marijuana. Things heated up quickly, and Anna got weepy. She dragged all of us to her bedroom and kneeled next to an oak hope chest. She proceeded to haul out baby clothes, dolls, and accessories she hoped to give to a daughter.

That was when J. Howard Marshall II called. He'd called many times during the evening, but Anna had refused to talk to him. This time she did but told him she wasn't feeling well and that she'd call him later. No mention of the party was made.

After hanging up, Anna led everyone outside, where Tim and Jeff had cranked up the jacuzzi. It was clear Alan was going to stay for the night, which was odd, seeing as how it was Christmas Eve and the man was married with children.

The tone of the evening changed from innocent fun to the beginnings of another night of wild partying as Anna and her guests stripped off their clothes and clambered into the hot tub. That's when we left.

Chapter 12

*A*nna continued to gain popularity as a *Playboy* Playmate. She received an extraordinary amount of fan mail, which would be forwarded to her from the magazine.

Al Bolt remembers her sitting on the floor surrounded by her mail. It was like Christmas. She would tear open the big packages first. Men would send her pictures and ask for autographs. Sometimes they would send taped messages to her.

Of course, she got letters from wackos, too. One guy thought she was an alien. But she tried hard to answer the letters, even though she continued to have trouble finding the words.

Things were not so rosy between Anna and us. She had changed considerably over the course of the year. Not only was she becoming famous, but she was becoming a *star*. At least, that's how she thought of herself.

Personal appearances were no longer the fun they'd once been. Anna was demanding, petulant, even rude. She wanted money, lots of it. She wanted to be the center of attention and not just in Houston. The *Playboy* cover was just the beginning, and once she'd spoken to Paul Marciano, she figured this was it. Her time. Her chance.

She had stepped into the media spotlight just as Alice had stepped through the looking glass.

Nothing would ever be the same.

She abruptly stopped calling us. When the contract-year expired, there was no discussion, no goodbyes. Anna managed herself for awhile, getting help from Melissa Byrum, the woman from the car show in Ohio who had taken part in that bizarre trip to New Orleans. And she had signed with Elite Modeling in New York at about the time of Guess? breakthrough.

She was on her way out of Texas, and as long as someone, anyone, could tell her the difference between New York and California, she was ready to circumvent the globe.

Chapter 13

*A*nna Nicole and J. Howard Marshall II went public in the beginning of 1992. He took her to his favorite haunt, the River Oaks Country Club, often. Of course, she was living in the house he bought for her, and each time she saw Howard, money exchanged hands.

It wasn't until 1993, however, that the big money on jewels started to come to light.

In March 1993, Marshall bought Anna over $100 worth of Godiva chocolates and more than $350,000 worth of jewelry from Neiman Marcus. Only a month later, the couple went to New York City and made a stop at Harry Winston's. Marshall was in his wheelchair, and Anna was in heaven.

According to one salesperson, Anna was "allowed to pick out whatever she wanted." That included a two-carat diamond ring, a round diamond ring, a marquise diamond ring, a diamond neck-lace, a pearl-and-diamond necklace, a diamond bracelet, a pair of diamond ear clips, and a pair of pearl-and-diamond drops.

Texas Monthly, in its October 1993 issue, reported that all this shopping took place in under an hour. The tab? Two million dollars. Paid for with a platinum American Express card.

Of course, Marshall had a track record for being generous with his mistress—until death did them part.

Chapter 14

The press watched everything Anna Nicole did and reported it to the world. She was called a supermodel, a starlet, a phenomenon.

On June 15, 1993, she was Larry King's guest on his CNN television show. Dressed in a blue-and-white polka-dot halter-top dress, with her hair done a la Marilyn, she was stunning. It was clear Larry King thought so.

Anna told the story she'd rehearsed over and over again. How she'd sent Polaroid pictures to *Playboy*, how she'd been whisked out to California and onto magazine covers, how Paul Marciano had turned her into the Guess? girl.

The questions didn't matter and neither did the answers. Anna Nicole was utterly charming. She called Larry "sir," and even after he asked her not to, she repeated the honorific several more times. She was nervous, that was easy to see, but that just added to the picture. He asked her about her weight, she told him that she's big but wouldn't tell him her size. It didn't matter. He was under her spell.

It was difficult to pose nude, she said. She didn't get to see her son often enough. She wanted to tone up, not lose weight. She'd always looked up to the *Playboy* models. Her grammar was awful, and that, too, added to her charm.

The first caller was a woman. She told Anna she was beautiful, earning a delicious smile. Then she said Anna was a role model for women who aren't thin. Anna Nicole got serious and told the caller that there were times she'd been depressed about being so large, but now she loved her weight.

The second caller was another woman, and she also praised Anna for being a full-figured woman. Anna told of the many modeling agencies who asked her to lose weight. Her smile grew a bit evil.

Larry asked about this reaction from women. Anna confessed that women had always been mean to her before.

It ended too quickly. Anna was on a roll. She looked like she could take on the world. The camera focused on that million-dollar face. She smiled.

Inside Edition did a story on "The hottest model in the world right now—Anna Nicole Smith." Open any magazine, the host said, and you'll see her.

Marilyn Grabowski from *Playboy* talked about her magic. Old schoolmates recalled that she was just a small-town gal, nothing much to look at. One old friend, Jo Ann Hughes, marveled that one day Anna was living on peanut butter, the next on Dom Perignon.

Anna Nicole had this and several similar photos, shot on top of her baby grand piano, blown up to 40" x 60" size as a Christmas present in 1992 for her future husband, eighty-seven-year-old J. Howard Marshall II.

Vickie Lynn (bottom right) with brothers Donald and David and sister Shauna

Mother Virgie Hart, a Harris County (Texas) deputy sheriff

Cedrick Franklin
Nathaniel Gamble

Missy Gore
John Glover
Lisa Gregory
Jennifer Griffin
Ramonita Harris
Nikki Hart
Clay Hawkins
Nile Hawkins
Carmen Haynes

Sophomore Anna, who was using the name Nikki Hart, pictured in the 1985 Mexia High School yearbook

After dropping out of school, Anna Nicole worked at Jim's Krispy Fried Chicken.

Anna Nicole was Vickie Lynn Smith when this picture was taken with her baby son, Daniel.

An ad for Gigi's Cabaret, where Anna danced topless as "Miss Houston's Hot Robyn"

Some of Anna's friends from her "titty bar" days

Colleen Rafferty

Terri Cobble

April Story Richardson

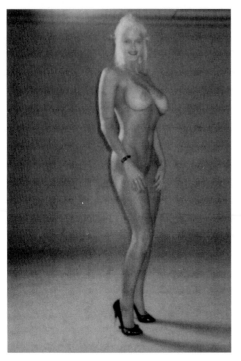

Eric Redding's Polaroid test shots of the then-Vickie Smith that caught the interest of *Playboy* magazine.

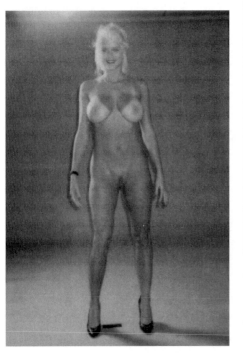

A different type of shot—a mug shot— taken by the Houston Police Department after Vickie Lynn Smith was picked up for Driving While Intoxicated, September 21, 1989.

Anna doing a publicity stint at the Silverado Club to preview her March 1992
Playboy cover.

Virgie Hart with Al Bolt at a benefit honoring the Houston Firemen Calendar Men.
Virgie bought a dance with Bolt for $75, which greatly displeased her daughter.

Anna with Warren Moon, former Houston Oilers quarterback. She wasn't happy posing with Moon because, she told Eric Redding, she "couldn't stand black men." Not long afterward, she began an affair with her black bodyguard.

With Houston Oiler linebacker, Ray Childress, who wasn't thrilled about appearing with Anna Nicole.

Daniel, duded up in cowboy attire, in a test shot for Guess? jeans. He didn't get the job.

Daniel with mom, Anna Nicole, enjoying some quality time.

Anna insists that if she treats Daniel "like an adult and keep him around in adult situations, he will mature quicker." Here Daniel watches Anna autograph her 1994 Landmark pinup calendar.

Cousin Melinda Beall, Aunt Kay Beall's daughter.

Kay Beall's back with a tattooed likeness of Anna Nicole. Anna begged Kay to get the tattoo to demonstrate her "true love and affection."

Polaroid shots of Anna taken by
Eric Redding over the years

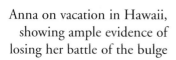

Anna on vacation in Hawaii,
showing ample evidence of
losing her battle of the bulge

With boyfriend/bodyguard Pierre DeJean.

J. Howard Marshall II and Anna Nicole on their "honeymoon" in Bali, April 1994, several weeks before their June 27 wedding.

They showed Anna with Hugh Hefner, getting her $100,000. They showed her with her new Jaguar. She told the camera that she's getting back at everyone who was ever mean to her. "I'll take all I can get."

E!Entertainment did a show on supermodels. Anna stood alongside Cindy Crawford, Lauren Hutton, Isabella Rossellini, Iman, Elle Macpherson, Christie Brinkley, and Kate Moss.

Anna talked about how hard the work is. Her number one tip? Be real bubbly and have fun.

Arsenio Hall had her on his show. She wore a black jumpsuit and dwarfed the host. She told him how much she wanted to meet Brad Pitt. How she liked her newfound fame. How she preferred men who were not too big or too small and looked at his hand to see how he measured up.

It was Virgie's birthday, and Anna told her "I love you, Mommy," right there on camera. The audience ate it up.

Inside Edition reported that Anna Nicole nearly started a riot in Hong Kong. She's revered there as a goddess. But, she told the reporter, she would never appear nude in a movie—unless she had the starring role.

*A*nd then the days of magic were over. It was just that fast. For a few brief moments, she was the golden girl basking in the golden rays of the media sun. It started to get overcast with the news that she'd been hospitalized for a drug overdose.

*I*n February 1994, *People* magazine reported that she and a twenty-year-old male friend, Daniel Ross, were hospitalized in Los

Angeles for what police described as an overdose of prescriptions drugs and alcohol. Anna's publicist said she went to Cedars-Sinai Medical Center suffering from a severe migraine.

However, people close to her disclosed that security guards found Anna sprawled naked on the bed in a Beverly Hills Peninsula Hotel suite, along with Mr. Ross. They also found smashed vases, overturned chairs, and torn photos.

Anna was at the hotel, in the $1000-a-night suite, because her home, one previously owned by Marilyn Monroe, had been damaged by an earthquake.

According to *Globe* magazine, "Anna drank an entire bottle of tequila on her own. She also took eight tablets of Vicodin and seven Xanax."

A staff member of the hotel told one reporter that Anna and Daniel had been in the hotel lobby the night before, embroiled in a screaming match. They had been drinking Sex-on-the-Beach, a vodka-based concoction, and plenty of them.

"Then he ordered some cigarettes and Anna started nagging him about his smoking," the hotel employee told the *Star*. "She was saying she didn't like the way it made her hair smell, and she wouldn't kiss him because he had bad breath."

Ross went to another part of the bar, and some other guy took the opportunity to make a move on Anna. That's when Ross started yelling. A shoving match almost turned into a fistfight, but Anna ran to her room with Ross in pursuit.

The *Star* article claims that Anna had a purse full of prescription drugs, including Imipramine, temazepam, Aldactazide, Decdron, Methocarbamol, Prilosec, Propulsid, Paxic, Seldane, Synthroid, and Vicodin.

It was Ross who alerted the front desk and asked for a cab to take him to a hospital. Paramedics were dispatched, but by that time, hotel security had found the unconscious Anna.

One witness said, "She sure didn't look like a supermodel," as Anna was wheeled out to the ambulance. "Her hair was sticking up straight like a broom, and her makeup was smeared all over her face."

Ross was reportedly in no better shape. He was taken to the Century City Hospital, and by the time he arrived, he was in convulsions. His heart rate was over 160, and he was listed as critical.

Both Anna and Daniel told police that the overdoses were accidental, that they didn't realize mixing drugs with alcohol could be so dangerous.

Chapter 15

*A*nna has always been a woman driven by her appetites. Not just food, not just champagne, not just sex, but all of them, all the time.

Clay Spires, the man who had been her boyfriend beginning in January, 1990, then, shortly thereafter, her bodyguard, told the *Globe* that J. Howard Marshall II had called many times while he and Anna were making love. "She'd tell me to keep quiet while she talked to him."

That same story was told by Al Bolt, another ex-boyfriend. He was also told to "hush up" when "Paw-paw" called.

Clay also came forward with stories of Anna's relationships with women. He talked about a Sandra Powledge, whom he claims was Anna's lesbian lover. Once, he told reporters, he witnessed Anna and Sandy, naked in bed together, painting each other's toenails.

Astonishingly, Clay also claimed, in the November 14 issue of the *Globe*, that Anna Nicole drugged J. Howard Marshall II to hide her lesbian lover!

"In fact," Spires said, "when Mr. Marshall came out to California...I think Anna Nicole tranquilized the old gentleman—because she put him to bed and locked the door to the bedroom she was sharing with [another lesbian lover] Susie."

He told us that there were many threesomes. Sometimes he would watch, sometimes he would participate. It was something both he and Anna enjoyed.

"She got drunk just about every night I was with her," Spires continued. "She also regularly abused drugs. She's really into painkillers and also likes an illegal amphetamine called Ecstasy."

One time, he recalled, she got so spaced out on booze and drugs that she "thought she was getting sucked into a picture of Marilyn Monroe."

Food, an addiction Anna has battled most of her life, was just another substance she abused. Clay talked about the whipped cream, waffles, burgers and fries, candy, ice cream, in never-ending supplies.

Of course, after these excesses, Anna would throw up and take great quantities of laxatives. Just like so many bulimic women in this country, Anna was convinced that she had to be at her "fighting weight," which was quite large according to Hollywood standards, and that she would do anything to stay that way—except, perhaps, eat properly.

Anna has had at least two liposuction procedures, each one causing her tremendous pain and discomfort, only to begin eating great quantities days after the surgeries. Melinda Beall, Anna's young cousin, accompanied Anna to her first liposuction treatment and recalls that she was so bruised afterwards, she couldn't drive for two weeks.

"We had to wait on her hand and foot," Melinda said. "She thinks now that she got her liposuction, she can eat donuts and cakes. We bought her a cake—she ate the whole thing in less than twenty minutes. It had icing piled up high, it was a little teddy bear made of frosting. In a month, Anna had gained all the weight back that she'd had liposuctioned out. Twenty-five thousand dollars, right down the drain."

Melinda, who always worried about Anna's unhealthful habits, feels that "Anna just wants to look good. She cares about the money, I'm sure, but she really just wants to be popular. All of her life, she wanted that. Because in school, she was a nerd. She was a terrible nerd. Nobody liked her. Billy Smith was the only date she had."

Well, she'd gotten her wish. She was popular. She was a celebrity. She was someone.

But at what cost?

Cocaine to keep the appetite quashed, amphetamines to do the same. Binging and purging. Using laxatives. And then the Vicodin, Xanax, Demerol, Imipramine, Temzepam, Aldactazide, Decadron, Valium, Seldane, and on and on. A prescription for big trouble if there ever was one.

Chapter 16

When Anna first went to Los Angeles, she moved into a house that had once belonged to Marilyn Monroe.

Anna became convinced that she was Marilyn reincarnated or that she was Marilyn's illegitimate daughter. She had pictures, posters, memorabilia spread all over the house. Her friends and relatives knew that a Marilyn poster was always a gift that Anna would love.

Unfortunately, she didn't love the house itself. It wasn't in good shape, and it was very plain. The pool didn't even have a heater. The first big earthquake that came around made the house almost uninhabitable, and Anna finally gave it up.

She moved to Brentwood—a very high-priced section of Los Angeles. It became famous—or perhaps more correctly, infamous—as O. J. Simpson's neighborhood.

Anna's new house was a two-story contemporary with four bedrooms. The master suite for Anna, one room for Marshall, one for Daniel and his nanny/companion Sam, and one that Melinda liked to call her own.

The pool in Brentwood was most definitely heated. As was the jacuzzi. And the landscaping was something of a dream—roses, roses, everywhere. Inside, outside, on the walls, and in the kitchen.

Anna had her Marilyn pictures hung in the new house, but they were far outnumbered by those of Anna.

While Anna loved the house, the atmosphere, the city, her son Daniel wanted nothing more than to go back home, to Houston.

According to Melinda, "He's got four earrings in his ears. Anna told him that she wasn't going to give him dinner unless he got his ears pierced. So he got four earrings. Two on each side. I think it's ugly. And so is his hair. It's really long, and he said he looked like a girl."

His room was filled with toys, including his favorite—Nintendo. But the best thing Daniel had was Sam.

Nassir Samirami was something of a surrogate everything to Daniel. He got the boy to school, made sure he was fed properly, dressed properly, and to the best of his ability, he tried to keep Daniel happy.

"Sam is a good man," Kay Beall told D'eva. "He takes him to school and does everything for the child. He's the only one that [Anna's] never slept with. He's the only one I really liked for Daniel to be with all the time because I know he won't hurt Daniel. Anna pulls away from everybody that gets close to Daniel. If you show him too much love and kindness, she thinks you want something for it."

Chapter 17

*I*t is our understanding that on or about June 2, 1992, Maria Antonia Ceratto was hired by you as a housekeeper and caretaker for your son Daniel Smith. Our investigation reveals that Ms. Ceratto has a cause of action against you for each of the following particulars as a result of your actions which occurred while in your employment, including but not limited to:

a) sexual harassment;

b) sexual assault;

c) false imprisonment;

d) conversion; and

e) intentional infliction of emotional distress.

As previously stated, Ms. Cerrato was hired as a housekeeper and caretaker. Shortly after the commencement of her employment, she *became aware that in addition to the numerous relationships you had with men, you also had sexual affairs with women. Although these activities bothered Ms. Cerrato, she needed her job and decided to continue her employment as long as you did not bother her.*

In the months that followed, you repeatedly asked her to accompany you in the evenings and she repeatedly refused. In addition, you showered her with gifts and told others that you were in love with her and found her attractive. Even though Ms. Ceratto informed you that she was not a lesbian and would not participate in such activities, you continued your advances and encouraged her to break her engagement so that you could "have her all to yourself."

Because of her fear of losing her job, Ms. Ceratto endured your embarrassing and humiliating treatment. These events ultimately led to your sexual assault of an intoxicated Ms. Ceratto in a hotel room in Las Vegas, Nevada. After forcing yourself upon Ms. Ceratto, you made many false promises, including the promise to marry her, so that she would continue to submit to your sexual demands.

As you are aware, Ms. Ceratto speaks very little English. Because of this language barrier, you were able to keep Ms. Ceratto a virtual prisoner in your home. You refused to allow her to go out or to have guests, and changed the phone number to prevent her communication with others.

Due to your acts and/or omissions, Ms. Ceratto has endured extreme mental anguish in the past and will continue to experience mental anguish in the future. By forcing Ms. Ceratto to leave without her possessions, you caused her great economic hardship. Ms. Ceratto was completely dependent upon you for her livelihood and support while in California, which allowed you to unjustly detain her. Furthermore, you sexually assaulted Ms. Ceratto when she was intoxicated and unable to defend herself against your advances. You then continued to force her to submit to your sexual advances out of fear of losing her job.

This letter is to serve as notice that a lawsuit will be filed on behalf of Ms. Ceratto if this matter is not resolved within thirty (30) days. Prior to the expiration of the thirty day period, this claim can be settled for the sum of TWO MILLION AND NO/100 DOLLARS ($2,000,000.00).

The letter went out February 3, 1994. Maria had found an attorney who would work on a contingency basis, Martha Garza. At the time this letter was served, Anna was embroiled in another fiasco that looked like it, too, was leading to a lengthy legal hassle.

The Ceratto accusation was one more piece of bad publicity that she just didn't need. She'd lost two years of the Guess? contract because of all the negative press, the opportunity to read for the Marilyn Monroe part in the remake of the movie *Niagara*, and now her agent Monique Pillar at Elite was telling her that Conair was canceling her contract.

According to the original petition filed in Harris County, and Anna's own testimony, Anna hired Maria Antonia Cerrato on May 6, 1992, as a caretaker for her son, Daniel. Anna's friend Debbie Hopkins had in her employ a woman named Blanca—Maria's sister. Even though Maria didn't speak English and Anna spoke no Spanish, they both felt the match would be a good one. No contract was signed, no agreement written. Maria was supposed to clean the house, look after Daniel, take him to school and activities, cook for him, and generally be responsible for the house and the boy on an ongoing basis. For this she received $200 per week, paid mostly in cash.

According to Ceratto's suit, Anna began sexually harassing her soon after her employment. Because she was a Honduran native and had limited use of English, Ceratto claims she didn't fully understand what was happening. It was only after Ceratto claims she witnessed a sexual encounter between Anna and another woman that the light dawned—she became aware that Anna was making sexual advances toward her. Cerrato then proceeded, as best she could, to tell Anna that she was not a lesbian and would not consent to a lesbian relationship.

Even though Maria said she wasn't interested, she maintained that Anna continued to sexually harass her, culminating on May 6, 1993, with a sexual assault by Anna in a hotel room in Las Vegas. According to Ceratto, Anna insisted that she accompany her to a nightclub that evening. During the night, Anna also insisted that Maria have several drinks and take drugs, all of which, Ceratto claims, Anna provided. Then, after returning to the hotel, Anna forced herself sexually upon Maria, who was so severely intoxicated at the time that she was unable to defend herself.

Because of Maria's embarrassment and humiliation that she'd been a victim of a homosexual assault, and out of fear of losing her job, she continued to endure a sexual relationship with Anna for approximately six months. Maria contended that because Anna was a famous model and actress, no one would believe her if she reported the assault. Besides, she was dependent on Anna for her livelihood and couldn't afford to lose her job. Without a recommendation from Anna, Maria knew she wouldn't be able to get work elsewhere.

According to Maria, Anna had complete control over her life keeping her financially and emotionally dependent upon her. During this time, Maria states, Anna continued to have sexual relationships with other people: men and women.

It didn't end there. Maria Ceratto, in her statements to her attorney, claimed that Anna had told her numerous times that she was in love with her and wished to marry her. That Anna had given her clothes, jewelry, and other gifts, including a car. This to ensure that Maria would continue to "endure" Anna's unwanted sexual advances and to keep Maria quiet.

She states that from May 1993 until November 1993, Anna kept her as a virtual prisoner. Maria was not allowed to go out alone and could only leave when accompanied by Anna, or Sam, who was then Anna's chauffeur. Maria claims that she was not allowed to use the telephone and that Anna had her phone number changed to prevent Maria from receiving phone calls.

Then, according to testimony, Maria alleges that on November 7, 1993, at approximately 12:30 A.M., Anna instructed her chauffeur/bodyguard Nassir Samirami to order Maria out of the Los Angeles house. Maria was not allowed to remove any of her belongings. The police were called to make sure nothing at all was taken from the home.

That was Maria's version. Anna tells a very different story.

Chapter 18

According to Anna's deposition of January 17, 1995, Maria was very sweet, a very good person when Anna hired her. Then in September of 1992, things began to change when Maria befriended a girl named Angie. Anna maintained Angie began to influence Maria negatively, that Angie tried to get Maria to come on to Anna and to hug and kiss her and to ask Anna to marry her.

The first incident occurred in a Mexican restaurant in Houston, and Anna says she was quite shaken by the event and informed Maria that she didn't want Angie to come around anymore.

Things calmed down then and Anna bought a car for Maria for the express purpose of taking Daniel to school and doing other household chores. Anna signed the car over to Maria so that she wouldn't be liable in case of an accident. Anna also bought Maria a television set because the girl didn't have one in her room. The only other gifts Anna gave to Maria were little trinkets and knick-knacks from airports and gift shops, which were given as tokens.

Anna had been very pleased with Maria's attention to the house and to Daniel until one afternoon when she, Maria, and Angie went to lunch at a Mexican restaurant in Houston. They all had a lot to drink, and Anna claims that Maria tried to kiss her right there in the booth. Maria pointed to her ring finger and in broken English asked, "You marry me." Anna quickly finished her meal and drove Maria and Angie back to her house. When Angie left, Anna told Maria that she didn't want the woman back in her home, ever again. The restaurant incident only compounded Anna's previous suspicion of Angie, whom, she said, she'd found rifling through her mail on several occasions.

Nothing untoward happened for awhile, although Anna was not pleased with the number of long-distance calls Maria was both making to and receiving from a boyfriend. That came to a head when the boyfriend called the house very late one night and woke Anna and Daniel. Anna told Maria then that the long-distance phone calls had to stop—no more calls to the boyfriend, no more calls from him.

Shortly thereafter, Anna moved to Los Angeles, to the Marilyn Monroe house, bringing Maria along with her. The move itself went smoothly, but the situation with Maria began to deteriorate quickly after that.

Anna noticed first that Maria had begun to neglect her chores. The house was no longer clean, and according to Anna's deposition, "There were spider webs all over." Second, she saw that Maria had begun to drink. White wine was the libation of choice and supposedly Maria went through quite a bit of it.

Anna later learned from her chauffeur that while she was away on business, Maria used a limousine service, charging nearly $25,000 in fees to Anna over a period of six months. Also according to Sam, Maria would frequently rent X-rated videos, lesbian videos, and charge them to Anna.

Daniel was left with others more and more frequently. The wholesome meals Maria used to cook were replaced by fast food and microwaved meals.

Then, in the summer of 1993, Maria began drinking wine during the day, and she encouraged Anna to join her. During one two-week period, Anna testified that Maria kept her intoxicated while feigning her own drinking.

According to the deposition taken on January 17, 1995:

Attorney Todd N. Moster: So she [Maria] was giving you drinks?

Anna Nicole Smith: Yeah.

Moster: Okay, so she offered you a drink that night and you had a drink?

Smith: Right. She offered me drinks many nights, but this night I did have a drink.

Moster: Okay.

Smith: Because, you know, I can't drink when I'm working because the next day my eyes are—I'm out of it. I can't work.

Moster: Okay. So you had a drink that night because she offered you some white wine.

Smith: Right. And I didn't have to work the next day.

Moster Then what happened?

Smith: Then 8:30 in the morning [I] got up. She was drinking. She offered me some more to drink. I was drinking. We ended up drinking all day.

Moster: Why did you drink with her all day?

Smith: She just kept begging me. She said, "Come, Bicky, please, please. Bicky, please, please, please." But what I was noticing is she was not drinking.

Moster: She was not drinking.

Smith: No. She would have the same glass. She was feeding me.

Moster: So what happened after you started drinking?

Smith: I went and got in the jacuzzi. Okay. She was not drinking. She was putting hers back and kept bringing me drinks, bringing me drinks.

Moster: How do you know that Maria wasn't drinking?

Smith: Because Sam was watching her. I passed out in the jacuzzi.

Moster: You went into the jacuzzi and you passed out?

Smith: I passed out cold.

Moster: Then what happened?

Smith: She took my clothes off, my bathing suit. Sam said that I was passed out, so I don't know what happened. Okay? Sam told me— okay. Billy, he works for Playboy, he does lights. So he comes out there. Billy's worried. He goes and tells my boss, you know, I'm in trouble the next day.

Moster: Okay.

Smith: Sam comes out, and he sees Maria come to me and start hugging me and kissing on me and putting her hands down there.

Moster: When you say "down there," you're talking—

Smith: Down in my personal, private area—

Moster:—genitals. Okay.

Smith:—that I don't let women touch. Sam said she was wearing a bathing suit top with nothing down there on.

Moster: So Maria was wearing a bathing suit top, but she was bottomless?

Smith: Right.

Moster: Did you see Maria or become awake during any of this time?
Smith: No. Sam put me to bed.

*T*wo days later, also according to the deposition, Maria got Anna drunk again. Anna's friend Alexis Vogel, a makeup artist for *Playboy*, went to the bedroom to say good night, and she found Maria "just trying to attack me."

"Maria's on top of me trying to take my clothes off, and Alexis is, like, 'Maria!' You know? 'Leave her alone.'"

This behavior, getting drunk and staying drunk, continued for about two weeks. Then, Anna reported she "snapped out of it."

A couple of weeks later, Anna claimed that she was taking a bath and Maria got in the tub with her, attempting again to kiss her and touch her. Anna left the bathroom shaken.

Maria asked Anna to marry her a month later. According to Anna's testimony, both she and Maria were sober at the time, and Maria pointed to her ring finger and said, "You marry me."

Finally, in December of 1993, while Anna was back in Texas, she received a late night phone call from Maria. Anna was recuperating from surgery at the time and had left Maria to take care of Daniel in Los Angeles.

It was two in the morning, and Maria was intoxicated. She wanted to go out. Anna yelled at her then, telling her she couldn't go out, that she couldn't leave Daniel.

Maria then said, "Me no more wanna work here."

Anna said, "Fine. Get out." Then she called Sam and asked him to get over to the house immediately.

When Sam called Anna back, he said that Maria had some people there, in a brown car. She was loading Anna's stereo in the car. She'd already loaded clothes and jewelry, all of which were Anna's.

When Sam demanded Maria return the property, Maria tried to hit him. At that point she went to Daniel's room and packed some clothes before waking up the boy. According to Sam, Maria told Daniel, "I'm taking you to Honduras."

Sam wouldn't let her take Daniel, and at this point, he called the police. Two officers arrived in about fifteen minutes. After hearing Sam's explanation of the situation to them, they contacted Anna, who told them, "She's trying to steal my kid. She just quit. I want her out of my house. I don't want her to take not one thing."

The brown car had left before the police arrived, and it's not clear what was in the trunk. According to Anna, the stolen goods included her cellular phone, thirty-thousand-dollars worth of clothes, her stereo, and hundreds of dollars worth of jewelry.

The police prevented Maria from taking anything else. They couldn't arrest her, but they could and did take the house keys. According to the police officers, Maria told them she and Anna were having a "lover's quarrel."

Once Maria was gone, Anna hired Sam on a full-time basis to take over the care of Daniel.

Maria filed suit two months later.

Chapter 19

*T*he December 1993 issue of *People* ran a short clip about yet another lawsuit. This time it was her ex-publicist, David Granoff. He claimed she walked out on her one-year contract with him after only five months and owed him more than $17,000.

Anna's contract with David Granoff Public Relations, Inc., signed April 16, 1993, called for Granoff to represent Anna for one year for a fee of $2000 per month. It also delineated the out-of-pocket expenses that would be borne by Anna Nicole. These included photocopies, transportation, telephone, postage, press kits, messengers, etc. Anna was asked to make a $500 deposit to cover these items on the day she signed the agreement.

The final statement for services, sent to Anna through her attorney at Irwin and Rowan, not only included seven months of back fees for $14,000, but also telephone, messenger services, press clipping services, and more, for a total of $17,143.13. The bill was dated September 9, 1993.

On December 2, 1993, Granoff filed suit with the Supreme Court, State of New York for breach of contract. In addition to the $17,000 outstanding invoice, the suit asked for no less than $500,000 in damages.

Oddly, the suit also included an order to pick up diamond earrings. Granoff says that on August 3, he received diamond earrings from Anna Nicole's former security agent for safekeeping. Granoff put them in a safety deposit box at the Chase Manhattan Bank in New York City. Although he repeatedly requested Anna to get the earrings, she had failed to do so.

*J*ust before Anna's big screen debut, her publicity machine went into high gear. *Los Angeles* magazine's Daniel Foster did a question-and-answer session with Anna in September.

When asked about her youth, Anna told the reporter, "I grew up in a small town, where there was totally nothing to do. All the kids would go up and down the drag and talk and drink beer. I did it, too—me and my friend Jo Lynn. Everyone in Texas drinks beer. I drink it when I go home. I've got a ranch there, where I can chase the chickens and pigs and play in the mud and run the horses. But I think Mexia is a place to grow up in and then retire. I don't think there's a middle."

Later, she talked of her husband, Billy Smith. How he was physically abusive and jealous and would never let her go out. "I thought," Anna said, "well, if I was to have a baby, I would never be lonely."

Foster then asked about her weight. About the fact that she'd been so thin as a girl and how she shot up to two hundred pounds after the birth of her baby.

"More and more women are coming out about their weight," she told him. "I get thank-you letters all the time. Or they stop me on the street and say, 'I'm so glad you're here—that you weigh as much as you do. Finally, there's a woman and not a waif'. I used to dress up like Marilyn Monroe. I have all her songs and movies. Most men, I think, like a womanly figure."

Finally, Foster brought up the subject of breast surgery. "I haven't had silicone implants," she said. "No."

*T*he April 1994 issue of *Houston Scene* magazine ran a short article about Anna Nicole. Impressed with her guest-starring roles in *The Hudsucker Proxy* and *Naked Gun 33 1/3: The Final Insult,* Earl Ditmman asked how it felt to be called an actress.

Anna replied that she liked to act but didn't like all the waiting inherent with movie making. She was confident that after people had seen her in both movies, that she'd be taken more seriously. Once again, she told the story of her outsized breasts being a result of gaining weight during her pregnancy.

She also hotly denied what had been printed about the episode with Daniel Ross, where she was rushed to Cedars-Sinai Hospital. The press had completely distorted what happened. "It hurt my feelings a little bit," she said of the coverage, "but I guess those guys just have to sell papers by making up stories."

*S*hortly after *Naked Gun 33 1/3* was released, the cast went on the *Phil Donahue Show.* It was clear that the other cast members were nervous about Anna's involvement, afraid that she'd say something embarrassing not only about herself but about the movie. Anna was also worried about the show, and one of her friends told Eric that she handled that by getting stoned. Xanax and cocaine—the breakfast of champions.

At a Las Vegas video show, Anna Nicole answered questions in a round-table interview. David Salcido of *Entertainment Weekly* commented that "The bosomy blond's screen debut in *Naked Gun 33 1/3* may mark the beginning of a whole new career. But as what isn't clear."

When asked what she liked best about making the film, Anna said, "Oh, me and Leslie [Nielsen] played around so much. Me and him were probably the funnest in the whole movie. Leslie was always using his fart cushion. He has this fart cushion, and he farts, and then he walks away. I was dying. I mean, I was just on the floor."

When asked where she saw herself in five years, she responded, "Well, I'm either going to be a very good, famous movie star and model, or I'm going to have a bunch of kids. I would miss having a career, but I've done my acting, and I've done my modeling. I've done everything I wanted to do. If no one wants me to be an actress anymore, well, I've made my goals. And if I don't work another day, I've done what I wanted to do."

At the Fifteenth Annual Razzies, Anna was awarded the Golden Raspberry Award for her performance in *Naked Gun 33 - 1/3*. Her title? Worst New Star of the Year.

O.J. Simpson was also awarded a Raspberry for *Naked Gun*, as Worst Supporting Actor.

Anna's Aunt Kay believes that her niece is a good actress. That "she can make a person believe." But she told Eric that her fondest wish is to have Anna get into a "mild movie, with [her] clothes on. I know she's getting tired of just being used for her body. That would aggravate anybody."

Chapter 20

*P*at Walker, the owner of the White Dove Wedding Chapel told a reporter for *Texas Monthly* that on June 25, an interracial couple in a black pickup truck came by and told her they wanted to book a wedding. Although they were wearing casual T-shirts, and didn't appear to be wealthy, they ordered the best of everything, which was the $1,000 package. The couple assured Walker that "Money is no object."

When Walker asked to see the marriage license, she informed the couple that they wouldn't be able to wed until Monday, the twenty-seventh. In Texas, there is a seventy-two-hour waiting period, and the license had been signed at 2:05 P.M. on June 24, 1994, at a Harris County courthouse.

On Monday, the bride entered the chapel wearing curlers. Someone asked Walker not to call any reporters. The bride told her

"I'm not marrying him for his money. He's been begging me to marry him for over four years. But I wanted to get my own career started first."

Finally, Walker turned to the bride and asked, "Who are you?"

Stunned, the bride said, "Well, I'm Anna Nicole Smith."

Walker's next surprise was that the handsome African-American, bodyguard Pierre DeJean, who had been with Anna Nicole constantly, was not the groom. The groom was to be none other than J. Howard Marshall II.

Anna Nicole wore white. A long, hand-beaded wedding gown, with train and a plunging neckline. The dress became more famous later when she wore it to Marshall's funeral service.

Daniel was there, of course, in a white tuxedo, acting as ring bearer. So were some of Anna's other relatives: mother Virgie, her aunt Elaine Tabers, and nieces and nephews. Anna was given away by a man she described at one point as her uncle and at another as her father. Marshall's nurse served as bridesmaid.

Finally, the groom entered. A small man in a tuxedo, a white shirt, and white shoes. Old enough to be the bride's grandfather. Her great-grandfather.

"I've done a lot of things," he told Walker. "I've made a lot of money. If I can make her happy, I've made her happy today."

Anna desperately wanted her groom to stand up during the ceremony, but when Pierre lifted him from his wheelchair, his legs simply buckled beneath him.

In the wedding book, under "How We Met," Anna Nicole wrote, "I was on stage. He was in the audience, and he was lonely and I started talking to him and we just started being friends." In reference to the 22-carat diamond wedding ring, she wrote, "This is the third ring I've had—the others were too small."

The chapel had been draped with white ribbons and white flowers. "She walked on white roses," Walker told *Texas Monthly*. "Not petals. Buds."

The music was "Tonight I Celebrate My Love for You." The groom was wheeled up the aisle. When it was over, two white doves were released from their cage.

Anna Nicole's aunt Elaine Tabers told the *Houston Press* that "It was real simple, but it was beautiful. A lot of people think it is strange, but their love is so strong it will put goose bumps on you."

Marshall reportedly told the eleven guests, all from Smith's side of the family, "I'm a millionaire. I've done everything I want to do in my life. Now, if I can take my money and see her spend it and get some of the things out of life and I can see it while I'm still living, I'll be happy."

A small reception was held in a room near the chapel. Anna Nicole, dressed in a wig, floppy hat, sandals, and a tight yellow suit, left from there to go to a photo shoot in Greece, leaving behind her brand-new husband, weeping in his wheelchair.

"Please don't *cwy*," she told him.

Then, she took Pierre DeJean's arm, waved bye-bye, and was gone.

Chapter 21

$\mathcal{T}$he press, of course, went wild with the news of the eighty-nine-year-old groom and the twenty-six-year-old bride. The age difference of sixty-three years is forty years more than the one between Jackie Kennedy and Aristotle Onassis. Thirty years more than the age difference between Woody Allen and Soon-Yi Previn.

David Letterman referred to Anna Nicole and her "situation" regularly in his Top Ten lists[1] all through 1995:

July 17, 1995:
"Surprises in the Mark Fuhrman Tapes" ...
4. Accuses O. J. of killing Anna Nicole Smith's husband

------

[1]Copyright World Wide Pants, Inc. All Rights Reserved

August 8, 1995:

"Items on the Westinghouse "To Do" List" ...

4. Have Anna Nicole Smith keep marrying rival network executives until they're all dead

August 15, 1995:

"Anna Nicole Smith Dating Tips"...

10. Forget the personal ads—try the intensive care unit

9. Wear something that, even to his failing eyes, will look slutty

8. Always carry some "mad money" for the paramedics

7. Make sure the valet parkers understand, if he dies in the restaurant, you get the car

6. When he wants sex, hide his glasses and put him in bed with a car battery

5. Remind him, "Hey, when you're 160, I'll be 101"

4. Prepare candlelight dinner. If he can blow out candle, you don't want him

3. To convincingly fake excitement during sex, just think about his stock portfolio

2. Good pick-up line: "Can I pre-chew that for you?"

1. Three words: "Bring extra plasma"

September 5, 1995:

"Things Overheard at the World Conference for Women"...

8. "Anna Nicole Smith sure seems to be warming up to Deng Xiao Peng"

September 11, 1995

"Excuses For Us Not Winning An Emmy" ...

4. Academy disapproves of my marriage to Anna Nicole Smith

November 15, 1995:
"My Retirement Plans"...
9. Bide my time 'til I'm 90; then marry Anna Nicole Smith

December 11, 1995:
"Good Things About a Cold Snap."
4. Husbands of Anna Nicole Smith stay fresher longer.

Yet those who know Anna well feel that this was not simply a matter of dollars and cents.

David Granoff, the New York publicist who brought suit against Anna for stiffing him, told London's *Arena Autumn* magazine that Smith talked about Marshall long before they were married. "She told me how he changed her life and how much she loved him and what a great person he was. She used to get calls from lots of people when we were travelling, but his calls she always took. Or if she couldn't take them, she would get a number and call him back as soon as she could.

"It was an unusual relationship but there have been stranger things in life than that. I do believe that she had great, great personal feelings for him. The money makes someone look a little better than maybe he would if they were not a high fashion model or a movie star but believe me, they had a real relationship."

Anna's cousin Melinda said, "She loved Howard. She did love him. Many people think that she's used him for his money, but it wasn't like that. I used to spend Christmas with them. It really wasn't like that. She took care of him. Howard really needed somebody. He was very nice."

People magazine, in an article on "Odd Couples and Peculiar Pairings" titled "Wedding Shockers," quoted Anna as saying, "I'm very much in love. I could have married him four years ago if I'd just wanted to get rich."

Of course, what most people wanted to know about wasn't love—it was sex. Just what did Anna do with a nonagenarian?

Several people, including Al Bolt, some of the girls Anna worked with in the bars, and eyewitness Pierre DeJean told us that Anna would bring home women, and they would have sex while Howard watched. She herself told Howard Stern that she would often take off her blouse and bra and rub her breasts on Marshall's head. Evidently, he got a big charge out of that.

*I*n response to questions about her recent marriage, she told reporters, "Well, he's an older gentleman. He's eighty-nine. I love him. He loves me. He asked me to marry him so many times, and I just wanted to establish myself first. I didn't want somebody to say, 'Aw, she married for money.' He was very sick. His girlfriend had just died. Right before that, his wife had died. He had no will to live. I saw him, I met him, and it was just like he was my friend. So we started going to dinner and to lunch. And he's helped me a lot. And the age difference—I don't care what people think. I love him, and we're in love, and that's it."

Chapter 22

$\mathcal{A}$nna Nicole's bliss at the event of her marriage might have been dampened somewhat had she known that J. Howard Marshall II had granted his son, E. Pierce Marshall, a living trust, originally dated September 1, 1982, and amended on June 23, 1992. According to the *Houston Chronicle*, two weeks after the marriage, Marshall signed control of his assets over to his son, as well as control over his life in a medical emergency.

According to the six-page power of attorney filed with the Harris County Clerk on July 15, Marshall signed over control of the living trust he established.

He also authorized Pierce to handle his business transactions. He transferred ownership of ten acres of land off Fenske Road near Rosehill-Cypress Road in Cypress, Texas, from the living trust to himself. The *Houston Chronicle* reported he kept the small ranch, valued at $960,000, for his bride.

Marshall had been estranged from his older son, J. Howard Marshall III, since the younger J. Howard had sided against his father in the dispute over control of Koch Industries.

This wasn't the first time Marshall signed over power of attorney to Pierce. In January, 1992, he signed a more limited document that he revoked in April of that same year, according to public records.

That document specifically authorized Pierce to handle litigation against his dead mistress, Dianne "Lady" Walker, and her children.

That lawsuit had been filed against Lady's estate in February 1992.

Marshall had given Lady more than $5 million in gifts, according to documents filed in federal court, as well as state court documents in Fort Bend and Harris counties. She had Rolls-Royces that matched her outfits and several dozen fur coats. Sources close to Lady said Marshall also paid for her last divorce.

In the 1992 lawsuit, Marshall sued Lady's estate and her children for the return of a condominium, 558,291 shares of stock in Presidio Oil, control of Colesseum Oil & Gas, and a portion of his life insurance policy he had signed over to Lady.

Just days after Lady died, Marshall wrote to Presidio, where he sat on the board of directors, and told them that the stock shares he gave Lady were "lost, stolen, or destroyed."

Presidio declined to reissue the stock, according to court records.

Whether he recovered the stock from Lady's estate is a secret sealed in the confidential settlement reached in 1993.

Public records indicate that the disputed condo ended up among Marshall's vast real estate holdings.

However, in October of 1995, a jury in Houston rejected claims that Marshall was a victim of conspiracy and fraud from Lady Walker. The jurors found the Marshall estate liable for over $200,000 in jewelry charges which it had refused to pay after Lady's death in 1991.

Kevin McEvily, attorney for the jeweler, said that he felt the estate, led by Pierce, was trying to get some of the money back that the old man had spent. The jury, however, felt that Marshall was competent when he bought the jewels and that he was responsible for the bills.

Chapter 23

The August 22, 1994, issue of *New York* magazine had an article, "White Trash Nation," by Tad Friend. Anna Nicole was on the cover, sitting on the floor, legs spread, with a package of Cheese Doodles between her legs. She's grinning through a mouthful of food, and still manages, despite the crass pose, to look beautiful. The cover copy reads, "Tonya. Lisa Marie. John & Lorena. Roseanne & Tom. Paula & Gennifer & Bill. They're everywhere. Lock up your Twinkies."

In the article "A Little Ol' Chat With Anna Nicole Smith," by William Boot, Anna is described as a "strapping country girl, come to town to be photographed," and that she is "absolutely unapologetic about the size of her breasts (enormous), her diamonds (enormous), her thighs (truly enormous), and her (enormously deep) twang."

When asked about her recent marriage to J. Howard Marshall II, she states unequivocally that, "I'm happy I did it. I'm very much in love with my husband. And he's very much in love with me."

Pierre DeJean, also present for the interview, commented that, "He's been askin' her for years."

Anna goes on with the story that she's told a hundred times before: that she didn't marry Marshall early on because she wanted to establish herself first. That she didn't marry him for the money. The picture inside shows Anna pointing to her 22-carat marquise engagement ring and diamond-studded wedding band.

Anna Nicole was incensed over the picture and the interview. She sued *New York*, claiming she'd been tricked. Although it's hard to understand how—she was smiling at the camera. Nonetheless, the suit was settled out of court, for something under $100,000.

By now, Anna had become a cultural icon. Jay Leno, David Letterman, Conan O'Brian all were taking potshots at her. The name Anna Nicole Smith had become synonymous with all the old jokes about women marrying for money. The quips don't need explanation—the country, the world—understands the significance.

She's also been made an icon, much as Oprah and Roseanne before her, as a woman of size. Of course, in this society that's a sin punishable by mass ridicule. In the August issue of *Esquire*, under the caption Things We'd Never Like to Say to a Woman We Love, is "Anna Nicole, do you really need that dessert? I can almost see the Statue of Liberty behind you."

Michael Musto interviewed Anna for *Entertainment Weekly*, just before *The Hudsucker Proxy* came out. The interview didn't cover much new ground but was used for fodder for countless magazine articles to come.

"Are you a feminist?" Musto asked.

"I don't understand that question."

"Do you fight for women's rights?"

"Whoever started that," Anna replied, "I could kick them in the head. I believe in women staying home and watching the children while the husband's at work—the traditional way. I would have been home with my family right now, except for my husband."

And her opinions about Sharon Stone and Madonna?

"She doesn't have a womanly figure," Anna said of Ms. Stone. On Madonna, Anna said, "She plays good music—that's *all* I can say. She should definitely stick to that."

In another spate of interviews, Anna decided to let her feelings about models be known. "I think thin models look so unhealthy," she told one reporter. "Who wants to hug a skeleton?"

"I wouldn't change my body for anything. Besides, I hate to exercise," she told the *Star*. "I just love sweets.

Chapter 24

On August 29, 1994, Pierre DeJean signed an employment agreement with Anna Nicole Smith. The contract, from the law firm of Myman, Abell, Fineman, Greenspand & Rowan of Los Angeles, was not just an employment agreement, but a confidentiality agreement.

The contract begins with, "You hereby expressly acknowledge and agree that Ms. Smith's privacy is highly valued and that you will make all efforts to maintain confidentiality with respect to all information and other material of any kind concerning Ms. Smith."

It goes on to specify that, "you shall not, at any time during the term of your employment or thereafter, use or disclose, directly or indirectly, to anyone any of the following described information: pictures, recordings, audio and/or visual tapes acquired by you in the course of or in connection with your employment by Ms. Smith...and all such information shall be deemed to be...private, secret and sensitive; and such information...shall not be removed or copied by you without Ms. Smith's prior written consent.

"Further, you shall not...give any interviews (whether oral or written), write or prepare or assist in the preparation of any books or articles.

"This letter agreement and the representations, warranties, covenants and acknowledgements shall be deemed to be a binding agreement between you and Ms. Smith and shall continue in full force and effect to the fullest extent provided under the law notwithstanding the termination of your employment."

The agreement was signed I. E. DeJean aka Pierre DeJean.

On October 4, *Star* magazine came out with a story that claimed that Anna Nicole was "living in fear of her bodyguard." The article states that Pierre, who's real name is Patrick Irwin, trashed her apartment in a rage. Police were called to Anna's Manhattan apartment at 8:30 A.M., on September 14 after neighbors complained about excessive noise, including screaming and smashing objects.

Witnesses reported that Anna Nicole was "covered in bruises as she fled."

When asked by a police officer if she needed help, she told them that Pierre, thirty, had "wrecked her apartment, throwing and breaking furniture while screaming at her at the top of his lungs."

"My ex-bodyguard, that is," she is quoted as saying.

No charges were leveled against DeJean, and Anna went immediately to Donald Trump's Plaza Hotel. Not just to his hotel, but into his arms.

Anna and Donald had dated before he wed Marla Maples. It was clear that the relationship was still cordial, as Trump "assured her he would keep her safe."

DeJean claimed, in several tabloid stories, that he and Anna Nicole had been lovers for more than two years, and that the incident at her apartment was nothing more than a lover's spat.

He told the *Star* "I never hit her, not once. She was bawling all night long and that's why the police were called. We are two people who love one another. The fact is, our relationship has happened. Nobody can take that away from us."

The *Star* tried to get a comment from Anna's representative at the William Morris Agency in Los Angeles but was refused a comment.

In the Newsmakers column in the *Houston Chronicle*, DeJean is quoted as saying, "She asked me to leave and I left. Every time we have a fight, she fires me. It's an emotional thing. Women are like that."

DeJean was fired after the episode in New York and decided that, regardless of the confidentiality agreement he'd signed, he was going to go public. On *Current Affair*, DeJean told viewers that he tried to leave, but Anna slapped him. He warned her to let it go, but she hit him again. He also claimed that he saved her life when she'd tried to commit suicide by slashing her wrists. He says that she was high on cocaine and that she begged him not to leave because she was in love with him.

The reporter called his claims outrageous and that it was hard to believe that Anna Nicole, this beautiful supermodel, had to force DeJean into having sex with her. DeJean's response? "Anna Nicole is a monster."

Of course, the reporter then told how Pierre DeJean is not his real name and that he'd served six years in San Quentin for manslaughter. It's painfully clear that no one believed one word the ex-bodyguard said.

Even so, DeJean didn't let it go. He made financial deals with several news groups, appearing full of outrage on camera. The charges grew with each show. He swore Anna forced him into a sexual relationship during her "honeymoon." He said he was constantly threatened. And, of course, the piece de resistance—he told reporters that she was carrying his child as she walked down the aisle.

"The deal was," he said, "the baby would be raised under J. Howard Marshall's name until he passed, God forbid, then I would be able to claim my own baby. Like a big dummy, I went along with the deal."

His assertions were called preposterous by Anna's attorneys. The reporter shook her head and turned to the next story.

We met with DeJean in February 1995, in Los Angeles. DeJean repeated the story about how Anna had planned to have his baby, but that the child would be adopted by J. Howard Marshall II. Anna, he claimed, wanted to make sure that she got more than her share of the money. DeJean was adamant that Anna had married Marshall strictly for the money, that love played no part in the transaction. He said that Anna had Marshall wrapped around her little finger and that Anna had told her aged husband that she was going to get pregnant somehow, but that he shouldn't ask her any questions. According to DeJean, all this was agreed to complacently by Marshall.

DeJean said that he and Anna planned on raising the child together after Marshall passed away, which they both knew would be soon. What hadn't been planned was the miscarriage, and that changed everything.

"I guess looking back," DeJean said, "it was stupid of me to even think that Anna would honestly have ever stuck by me in the relationship, or do what she said she was going to do...which was marry me after Howard was gone. We were supposed to raise our child and live happily ever after."

Another afternoon in Los Angles, DeJean arrived at the restaurant in a black Rolls Royce he claimed was a gift from Anna Nicole. He was dressed in black pants with a silver belt, black and gold Versace glasses, a white shirt, and a white headband. It came up early in the conversation that he speaks several languages: French, the patois of Jamaica and Haiti.

DeJean was quite upset at that lunch. It was December 1994, and he'd just been charged with stalking Anna Nicole. The Los Angeles Police Department had been called by Anna Nicole, who claimed that DeJean had phoned her numerous times, and threatened her.

Suspect (DeJean, Pierre) phoned Victim on above date and time and stated, "If I can't have you, no one will. I will kill you."

Suspect phoned victim's residence numerous times and demanded money and jewelry from Victim. Suspect also phoned Victim on above date and stated that he would be over [to] her residence to pick up his clothing. Victim terminated Suspect's services 9/1994 due to suspect's physical abuse towards her.

Witness 1 (Hazel Snyder) observed suspect knocking on Victim's door on 12-11-94 at approximately 1300 hrs. Witness 2, (Sam Nassir) Victim's current housekeeper, was advised of above incident and notified Bel-Air Patrol.

Witness 2 ordered Suspect to leave location. Suspect refused and stated, "I want to speak with Anna." Witness 1 is a neighbor of victim and observed above incident from her front lawn.

An emergency protective order was requested at Victim's location on 12/12/94.

The order was denied by Judge McBeh.

Also listed, as Witness 3, was Gerald (Clay) Spires. He gave Anna's address as his own but with a separate phone number.

Then on December 19, a complaint was filed with the Superior Court for the State of California by Anna Nicole Smith against Patrick Doe, a/k/a Pierre DeJean.

Case number SC034122 was a complaint for a temporary restraining order; preliminary and permanent injunctions, and damages for: 1) Harassment; 2) Extortion; 3) Intentional infliction of emotional distress; and 4) Breach of Contract.

Paragraph four of the complaint states: "In about February, 1994, SMITH hired DEFENDANT to act as a bodyguard for herself and her son. Thereafter, on or about August 29, 1994, in partial consideration for his engagement as a [sic] employee of SMITH, DEFENDANT executed a Confidentiality Agreement, a copy of which is attached hereto, made a part hereof and marked Exhibit "A." Pursuant to said agreement, DEFENDANT was contractually precluded from divulging or otherwise disseminating any information regarding any fact of SMITH's entertainment activities or personal life.

At about the time of SMITH's marriage to her present husband, in June of this year, DEFENDANT began to grow extremely possessive of SMITH and to make demands upon SMITH that were not appropriate for an employee. SMITH discovered that Pierre DeJean was not the DEFENDANT's real name and that the DEFENDANT had spent many years in prison for the commission of various violent criminal acts.

On or about September, 1994, while in New York on a modeling assignment, the DEFENDANT's behavior towards SMITH became increasingly threatening and abusive and ultimately resulted in his physical attack upon SMITH. SMITH immediately terminated his employment.

Subsequent thereto, beginning on or about October, 1994, and continuing to the present time, DEFENDANT has wrongfully and unlawfully engaged in a pattern of threatening, abusive and harassing behavior towards plaintiff, her husband and other members of plaintiff's family and household. DEFENDANT has made numerous phone calls to plaintiff's residences in Los Angeles, Houston and New York harassing her, threatening her physical safety and well-being, threatening the safety and well-being of plaintiff's husband and family, and demanding the payment of money. In addition, DEFENDANT has been caught trespassing on SMITH's gated property in Los Angeles, lying in wait for plaintiff's arrival.

DEFENDANT's acts of harassment include, but are not limited to, telephone calls of varying lengths commencing on or about September of 1994, up to and through the present; jumping the security fence around plaintiff's Los Angeles residence and lying in wait for her on December 11, 1994 in the early afternoon; and calling plaintiff on December 12, 1994 and stating "If I can't have you, no one will; I will kill you."

SMITH has repeatedly demanded that DEFENDANT cease and desist his threatening behavior and refrain from contacting SMITH or any member of her family or household. DEFENDANT refused and still refuses to refrain from his threatening conduct.

SMITH has suffered substantial emotional distress as a direct and proximate result of DEFENDANT's conduct; the same course of conduct would likely cause any reasonable person to suffer like emotional distress.

In furtherance of DEFENDANT's scheme and systematic strategy of harassment and blackmail, he has on numerous occasions made unlawful demands of money on SMITH under threats and duress specifically threatening to publish and disseminate defamatory and disparaging information regarding SMITH and her family all with a view towards overwhelming SMITH's will and judgment.

DEFENDANT's course of conduct has been outrageous and was performed with the intent to cause or with reckless disregard of the probability of causing SMITH's emotional distress.

A temporary restraining order was then issued.

Chapter 25

*D*eJean had a completely different story about the fight in New York that made the papers. Although Anna told reporters that he'd hit her, DeJean claimed that was completely untrue.

He said that Anna had come home very late that night, completely drunk. She told him that she'd misplaced her purse, which contained her credit cards and $7,000 cash. She asked DeJean to go back to two hotel rooms and ask if the occupants, whom she'd been with earlier, had found her purse. It was four in the morning, but DeJean did just that.

No one had seen the purse, and they didn't appreciate being awakened. By the time DeJean got back to the Anna's room, she'd found the purse. It had been with her coat all along.

DeJean was angry and wanted to apologize to the people he'd disturbed. Anna told him not to, to let it go. In fact, if he did apologize, he would be fired.

Anna then started to fight with DeJean, and he claimed that he never struck her. He did try to restrain her, especially when she grabbed a knife and threatened to slit her wrists. She managed to hurt herself but not badly.

After he'd patched her up with Band-Aids, he left. According to the story he told Eric, he walked to the Hyatt Regency Hotel and got a room. Once he was settled, he called Anna to make sure she was all right. Anna told him she was fine and that she was going to sleep.

According to DeJean, the next morning, he got a call from Carolyn, Anna's representative at Elite Modeling, who said he was in the papers, that's he'd beaten Anna.

DeJean said, that after he'd phoned Anna, she'd called Donald Trump. DeJean insisted that Anna and Trump had once been an item, that three years earlier they had been intimate friends.

When Eric asked him if it was true that Anna's room had been torn apart, DeJean told him yes, but that it was Anna who had done the tearing.

One last thing—Anna had been so angry at DeJean that she cut up his credit cards, canceled his flight home to Los Angeles, and made sure none of her people would help him. He had to ask a friend to lend him the money to leave New York.

Though DeJean told a nice tale, we had learned by that time to take everything he said with a grain of salt. Melinda had told us many times that DeJean was a bully, that she knew for a fact that DeJean hit Anna. On the other hand, we saw a Western Union telegram from Anna Nicole to Pierre DeJean, after the hotel incident, with $2000 dollars and a brief message. "I love you."

*T*hen there was DeJean's claim about Anna carrying his child on her wedding day. He had Marshall saying, "Yes, dear. Anything you say," after Anna told him she was going to get pregnant and he was not to ask questions.

Melinda and Aunt Kay reject this all as nonsense. Not only was Anna never pregnant with DeJean's child, Melinda has said Anna was afraid of DeJean. She was terrified of his temper and finally she ended up getting the restraining order to keep him away.

Kay Beall, who had known DeJean from the beginning told us that she wanted to "ring his neck." Shaking her head, she said, "I've met him and I don't know what to think about him. He tells me one story and a week later he tells me a different story."

"Was he telling the truth about Anna being pregnant with his child?"

"No. I was up there with Anna at that time. That child was not pregnant. She married Howard because Howard was a good man. I knew him. He was a wonderful man. Anna didn't even go to the hospital. She had her period. It wasn't a miscarriage. Just a normal period. You can tell him you asked Kay, and Kay said she was in the house with Anna. She knows the truth."

"Do you think Pierre actually beat her up in New York?"

"I wouldn't put it past him."

"Why do you think he's saying those things about Anna?"

"He's trying to scare her into giving him money. She got him a car to drive. The Rolls Royce. Also a white Mercedes. He just don't like it that his money's been cut off."

When D'eva asked why Anna had bought him the Rolls, it was Melinda who responded. "He wanted a Rolls Royce because he wrecked his. I got mad about that because she's never bought anybody in the family a Rolls Royce or anything that expensive. My

Aunt Virgie has to work three jobs. Two extra jobs just to make it. That's her own mother. If she would have given her the money for the Rolls Royce, my Aunt Virgie could have retired."

Chapter 26

*D*eJean, angry about the stalking charge, angrier about the fifteen thousand dollars in attorney's fees, fought as hard as he could to get Anna to back off. He had made tapes of Anna's phone messages and kept them. One call in particular was damaging to Anna's claim that she wanted DeJean kept away.

She'd had her phone number changed, and shortly after that, DeJean recorded the following message:

"Oh, honey, I miss you," Anna said, in that patented baby talk of hers. "Honey, I miss you and I really want to meet you, and here's my new phone number, but don't tell anybody I gave it to you."

This message was left in December, during the same period Anna claims, in her lawsuit, that she wanted nothing to do with DeJean.

DeJean was able to get the criminal charges against him dropped. He still had the threat of a civil case over his head, but he'd run out of funds.

Todd Moster, the attorney for Maria Cerrato had asked Eric to set up a meeting where he could meet DeJean. He wanted DeJean to testify on Cerrato's behalf, but DeJean refused. He was worried about the civil suit.

Another interesting slant came up about the tapes DeJean had made of Anna. She claimed that Pierce Marshall, Howard's son, was having affairs with two strippers. Anna was convinced DeJean could get their names, get some evidence she could use as leverage, given that Pierce held Howard's power of attorney. We listened to DeJean's tapes, and it was definitely Anna Nicole's voice on each one.

DeJean and Pierce had a meeting, also. Pierce showed up with three armed bodyguards. He asked DeJean to sign an affidavit stating that he'd had sexual relations with Anna Nicole before and after her marriage to J. Howard Marshall II. Money was offered, but DeJean would never say how much. He didn't sign the affidavit, and he didn't take the money, although he told Eric that perhaps he should have.

Oddly, during all of this, DeJean told D'eva that he still had strong hopes that he and Anna would reconcile.

They met, back when Anna was still going out with Daniel Ross, at a nightclub in Los Angeles called Tatou. DeJean and Ross knew each other, and after a long night of dancing and drinking, DeJean went up to Anna and whispered, "You were born and bred to be with a black man." Evidently, the line was quite effective, as later that night Anna got DeJean's phone number from Ross. She called DeJean several night's later and asked him to come to her home for an interview.

Their conversation must have been a good one, because later that same day DeJean was given keys to Anna Nicole's home and the job of bodyguard.

DeJean told us that he'd been a bodyguard since he left prison and that he'd worked for Zsa Zsa Gabor, Arsenio Hall, and Eddie Murphy. Eric discovered later that he, in fact, hadn't worked for Hall or Murphy.

DeJean also confided that his salary, while working for Anna Nicole, was $8,000 per month (although Clay Spires says that's nonsense—it was $2,000 per month) and that his employment ran from June of 1993 to January of 1994. Not only did he travel with her, he acted as her road manager. He was the man that went to Greece with Anna the night of her marriage to J. Howard Marshall II.

DeJean told us something fascinating not long ago. He respected J. Howard Marshall II very much, he said. They had had many philosophical discussions, during which J. Howard would recall conversations he'd had with Freud, Jung, and Machiavelli (who died in 1587)!

Chapter 27

According to many reports, including a piece in the January 24, 1995, issue of the *National Enquirer*, Anna spent that New Year's Eve at Hugh Hefner's big bash. After much drinking, champagne mostly, Anna jumped into Hef's swimming pool—fully clothed—at the stroke of midnight.

Guests were startled, to say the least. One unnamed attendee told the *Enquirer* that they were "surprised she didn't sink like a stone with that gigantic rock around her finger." Of course, that was a reference to the 22-carat diamond engagement ring Anna had gotten from hubby J. Howard Marshall II.

The *National Enquirer* titled their piece about the incident: Thar She Blows!

Clay Spires, her bodyguard and lover, also mentioned that after midnight, when Anna had dried off, that she and Judd Nelson went to the grotto and brought in the New Year with a bang.

Shortly thereafter, the media went on a feeding frenzy when Anna Nicole made her infamous stage debut with Bruce Willis at the opening of yet another Planet Hollywood, this one in San Diego, California. Anna's pictures, in the skintight red dress that had earned her a prominent place on most "Worst Dressed" lists, sang, cavorted, and of course, showed off the body that had made her millions. Several tabloids ran photos revealing Anna's naked breasts as they slipped out from underneath the tight garment.

It was reported that the Planet Hollywood publicist was quite unhappy with Anna's shenanigans, and that Demi Moore was furious at Anna's unabashed fondling of husband, Bruce, and that she insisted that Anna Nicole be barred from all future openings.

Next up was the debacle at the Academy Awards. Anna went to the ceremonies with Branscom Richmond, an actor who appears regularly on the syndicated television show *Renegade* and who also starred in Anna Nicole's last movie *To The Limit*.

Her comments to reporters were about her wedding—about how much she loved her husband. The reporters' reactions ran from amazement to revulsion. Everyone commented on her weight gain.

The pictures of Anna, larger than she'd ever been before, waving and smiling, wearing a skintight red gown, appeared in tabloids, newspapers, and magazines. She was ridiculed and pitied. It was a far cry from her debutante pose on the cover of *Playboy*.

Chapter 28

Only two weeks after the wedding, Howard not only gave Pierce power of attorney over his affairs, but amended the J. Howard Marshall II Living Trust, making it irrevocable and severing Anna from "the use and enjoyment of (its) assets."

After that, according to a lawsuit Anna Nicole filed, no one paid her American Express, MasterCard, and Visa bills. Also unpaid were her light and water bills, causing a termination of those services at her residences.

In September, challenges arose over the legality of presents Marshall had given Anna—a 1992 Mercedes, 1,000 shares of Campaigne Victoire, and the fifteen-acre spread outside Cypress, valued at $960,000.

At this point, Texas Commerce Bank refused to honor a $965,388.75 check Marshall had written to jeweler Harry

Winston. Winston sued Anna Nicole to either return the baubles or pay up.

By May 26, 1995, Marshall had grown unhappy with his son's efforts to restrict Anna's visits.

In her suit against Pierce, Anna included a statement by Marshall.

"Your honor, this is Howard Marshall. I am not a member of the Bar of Texas, but I am of two other states and the Supreme Court of the United States. I want you to know that I am perfectly competent. I think that my son Pierce has overreached a little bit in trying to make himself my guardian.

"I want my wife to be aided and supported by me. She's the light of my life. I don't think Pierce quite understands that. And maybe he's a little jealous."

On June 1, Anna pressed Judge Scanlan for the right to see her husband. She said she was not "permitted to stay in the home with Mr. Marshall longer than thirty minutes, after which time an armed officer indicates it is time for her to leave."

That rule appeared to have eased, court documents suggested, and the suit became mostly devoted to "discovery" matters as both sides continued to prepare for the courtroom.

According to Kay Beall, Marshall adored Anna. She remembers him saying that Anna was supposed to get money when he died. He wasn't crazy. He was very smart. But, Kay added, she didn't think Anna would ever see any of that money.

"Howard loved Anna and he wanted her to have that. It was his choice—not his son's, but Howard's. If she was trying to take it without Howard loving her, that would have been different. She went with Howard a long time. She could have married him years ago. He asked her over and over to marry him, but she wanted to get her career and her own money before she wed him.

"He was a sweet old man. There wasn't nothing that he would not do for you. He would ask you if you needed something."

Melinda also remembered that about Howard and that "He could eat three of those chocolates with alcohol in them and get drunker than a skunk. We used to laugh at him all the time."

"But Howard was always real supportive," Kay continued. "He always told [Anna] that she didn't have to work a lick if she didn't want to. He would tell her that he would take care of her, but she wanted her career.

"One thing, she was scared of him being old. Scared that he would get sick and she wouldn't know what to do. She always had Uncle Melvin or me or somebody there with her in case something happened. Melvin was real good with Howard. When they went out on trips, Melvin would go. He'd help him get up and get dressed. Up and down steps. They got along real good.

"I know for a fact that that old man just loved Anna with all his heart. I know that."

Chapter 29

$\mathcal{A}$nna Nicole went to probate court for the hearing on the guardianship of her husband on Thursday, February 16. Dressed in a simple flannel shirt and pants, her hair pulled back in a ponytail, wearing no makeup, it was clear to see that she was terribly upset by the proceedings.

Judge Jim Scanlan awarded E. Pierce Marshall temporary guardianship, despite Anna's entreaties. Pierce had petitioned the court for guardianship claiming that his father, J. Howard Marshall II, was mentally incapacitated. Basing his petitions on the reports from Dr. Stephen Rosenblatt, Pierce claimed that Marshall was cogent enough to answer direct questions by nodding his head.

Anna Nicole did come away with visitation rights, although someone from Pierce's camp was required to be present.

Pierce also made sure that his father's millions were put in trust, which, of course, guaranteed a lengthy, ugly lawsuit.

Anna was clearly devastated by the proceedings and went on television to talk about it.

In an interview with News 2 Houston, she said, "I'm not asking for millions and millions. I just want my bills paid and to have my salary back." Tear stained, wearing no makeup, her hair now in pigtails, Anna said of Pierce Marshall, "It hurts me, because I've kept his father alive for four years. He should be praising me. He should be happy. Howard told people that I saved his life. He has told me numerous times that I saved his life, and that he is here for one purpose—to take care of me and my son."

On the same day, in the same outfit, she told *Current Affair* that, "I could have been a rich snob. I did not marry him for his money. That's not me, that's not my character."

The reporter asked how Marshall's family viewed her. She replied that she couldn't say that on television.

"The most I worry about," she said, "is having to leave his side just to make money to live on, you know, I don't want to ever, ever leave him. I'm a total basket case, going to see my psychiatrist. I'm almost having nervous breakdowns all the time."

Anna also told the reporter that she took care of her husband in a "sexual way." She said that she did her "wife duties" even before they were married.

J. Howard Marshall's secretary was present during some of Anna's visits to the hospital. Several times, Anna brought Ray Martino with her. He'd directed two of Anna's films, *To the Limit* and *Skyscraper*. He wasn't above asking Marshall to put up some money for more films. He also made a point of putting rosary beads and crucifixes all over the room, telling Anna that he was trying to cast the devil from Marshall.

Kay also witnessed Martino's odd behavior. She was concerned when Ray started trying to get the "devil" out of Anna, as well as Marshall.

"He's not helping her by feeding her full of this devil stuff," she said. "That's not what she needs. She's not full of the devil. She's full of mischievousness, and she's mean sometimes. But she shows a lot of love. She's a lovable person. She don't need that Martino."

Chapter 30

*I*n July 1995, Anna and her entourage went to the Bahamas for a photo shoot—a topless one. Things went haywire when island security guards put a strong-armed stop to the proceedings.

The *Globe* reported, in its July 4 issue, that the two gendarmes, responding to complaints by other beachgoers, asked Anna to leave the beach. When she resisted, they "slammed her to the ground, then dragged her from the beach."

Anna Nicole was outraged. She told *Globe* reporters, "My whole life revolves around my breasts. Everything I have is because of them."

Interestingly, there is no law against topless sunbathing in the Paradise Islands. But something certainly stirred up the usually sanguine police.

Anna vigorously protested the police intrusion but was pushed to the ground for her efforts. Then, one of the native guards got her in an arm lock and dragged her off the beach.

Anna's publicist Tony Angellotti told *Globe* that Anna wasn't arrested, and no charges resulted from the incident.

As an aside, he also mentioned that Anna makes $18,000 a day for modeling, but the fee doesn't include bail.

What Anna didn't know, was that while she was being manhandled on the beach, Pierce Marshall was busy selling off some of Marshall's estate at auction in Houston.

Chapter 31

Jay Leno latched on to the Anna Nicole Smith story with a vengeance. For weeks, his monologues included at least one mention of the newlyweds:

"Did you hear about the twenty-six-year-old *Playboy* centerfold who married an eighty-nine-year-old guy? J. Howard Marshall II—I don't know how old the first is. The only thing they have in common is that they both grew up listening to the Rolling Stones."

"Now that Dole is seventy-one—that's an awkward age—too old to be on *Beverly Hills 90210,* but too young to marry Anna Nicole Smith. You remember her—she married an eighty-nine-year-old man worth five hundred million—and today, Tom Arnold proposed to both of them."

"She's twenty-six, he's eighty-nine—they had their first fight today over a sensitive issue. He wants to be cremated after he dies, she wants him cremated now."

"Let's strap Anna Nicole Smith in a lie detector and find out if she's really in love with that eighty-nine-year-old guy. That's what I want to know."

"I don't want to say he's old, but yesterday she told him to act his age—and he died."

"Anna Nicole Smith—you know her—in *People* magazine they show her with her eighty-nine-year-old husband. They want to have children. Hey Anna, to an eighty-nine-year-old guy, you are children."

"She did say they are more and more in love every day. She lives to hear him say those three little words...'I can't breathe.'"

"Last night in the monologue I did a joke about Henry Gonzales, the congressman from San Antonio. A rather elderly gentleman. Seventy-seven to be exact. I said he looked like the 2,000-year-old man, and today Anna Nicole Smith proposed to the guy."

"Anna Nicole Smith—you know who she is, right? She's the *Playboy* centerfold married to the eighty-nine-year old millionaire. In the paper today, she described their relationship. She said they're like two peas in a pod. You've seen the picture in *People* magazine? It's more like two cantaloupes and a prune. Please. Enough."

"Here's the oddball story of the week—I'm not making this up—twenty-six-year-old *Playboy* centerfold and Guess? jeans model Anna Nicole Smith, you know her? I'm not making this up. She's married to an eighty-nine-year-old Houston man who's worth something like five hundred million dollars. I'm not making this up. She married an eighty-nine-year-old guy. Here's my question.

Where does a twenty-six-year-old woman go to meet eighty-nine-year-old guys? You think she's bar-hopping with a bunch of girl-friends at some after-hours club, and she looks over and says 'Whoa, who is the guy with the aluminum walker? He is hot, yeah. Hey, whose teeth are on the bar, are they yours?' He's eighty-nine years old. Forget about sex—just carrying her across the threshold would kill him. Anyway, I guess they got married, spent their honeymoon alone, just the two of them alone up there in Niagara Falls, in the honeymoon suite, rewriting his will."

"Scientists in Europe have recovered the fossilized remains of a man reported to be 500 thousand years old...the man is half a million years old, and today, Anna Nicole Smith proposed to him. I heard about this, and just for fun I looked up the *Playboy* data sheets—under turnons, she said 'old geezers with bad hearts.' Now she's twenty-six, he's eighty-nine, she says she's happy taking her clothes off for a living, and he says he's happy if he's living after she takes her clothes off. It works out great. Actually, they were married last month, but just today he got her bra off. But she did say that he is an incredible lover, just incredible, all night long—of course, that could be the rigor mortis setting in, I don't know."

"The story we've been talking about all week—Anna Nicole Smith, anyone here from Texas? Ever hear of that guy? Is he famous? In the paper today, Smith called it a May/December romance—I guess she figures he may last till December. During the marriage ceremony, you think she laughed at the part 'Till death do us part?' Actually, there have been a few problems with the honeymoon couple. You know at first I understand that he was worried about how they would have sex, but I understand that she was very encouraging. She said, 'Don't worry, honey, about having sex. Where there's a will, there's a way.'"

"She says that he's a great lover, you know something? Every guy with 500 million bucks is a great lover."

On *Geraldo*, during his Friday afternoon gossip show, the wags went berserk. One tattler said, "God bless her. She found her sugar daddy."

Another complained that Anna wasn't giving any in-depth interviews.

Still another recalled a meeting with Anna at the Las Vegas Video Show. The reporter, a regular contributor to the *Star*, said Anna seemed very out of it mentally. Was it drugs?

Not one reporter regarded her seriously. In every way, they sneered, lifted their brows, snickered.

Jon Stewart did a parody on his late-night television program. He called it a one–woman show, "Anna Nicole Smith, Up Front and Beautiful."

"It is Texas, it is hot, and I am born," he said, wearing a skintight dress and a long blond wig. "I'm fifteen, and I will not fry chicken for the rest of my life, I want love. I want a baby. I want nice earrings. I want to be rich."

"Why, Mr. Hefner. Me? Pose nude? Why you could charm the honey out of the...things that makes honey."

"Wait, it's too much. Chicago, Austin, Beverly Hills, Jed, Ellie Mae, Xanax, are you gonna finish those fries?"

"I realized then that life is like a box of chocolates—and I'd eaten the whole damn box."

Chapter 32

J. Howard Marshall II died on August 4, 1995, at the age of ninety, in Houston's Park Plaza Hospital. His obituary, several columns long, ran in the August 9 issue of the *Houston Chronicle*.

"Mr. Marshall is survived by his third wife, the former Vickie Lynn Hogan (a.k.a. Anna Nicole Smith); son J. Howard Marshall, III and daughter-in-law Ilene Marshall of Pasadena, California; son E. Pierce Marshall, daughter-in-law, Elaine T. Marshall and grandsons E. Pierce Marshall, Jr. and Preston L. Marshall of Dallas."

Donations to the George School were requested in lieu of flowers.

His death caused yet another legal battle between Anna Nicole and Pierce.

Anna's attorney, Suzanne Kornbilt, said her client was adamant that Marshall's body be buried, preferably in a mausoleum.

Pierce wanted his father's body cremated.

171

In addition to the dispute over the remains, Anna's attorney filed suit to gain spousal support from the J. Howard Marshall II Living Trust. She wanted half his earnings since the marriage on June 27, 1994.

An employee at the office of attorney Diana Marshall, who also represents Anna said Anna wanted to use funds from Marshall's estate for her living expenses, which Pierce has managed to keep from her.

According to the *Houston Chronicle*, "Kornbilt acknowledged that Pierce Marshall's lawyers have done a masterful job at hamstringing Smith's every effort at utilizing her husband's funds. They likely will keep up their efforts at denying her a share in Howard Marshall's estate.

"'It's really up in the air what we'll be able to achieve in court,' Kornbilt said. 'They've been pretty mean about everything, but I think when this is over, the public will feel sorry for Anna Nicole.'"

Joseph S. Horrigan, attorney for Pierce Marshall, declined comment.

*T*wo funeral services were held for J. Howard Marshall II. Anna's private affair was held Monday, August 7, at Geo. H. Lewis & Sons chapel, complete with a white baby grand piano and candelabra.

Anna wore her wedding gown and veil. Her son Daniel wore a white tuxedo. A little black dog ran up and down the aisles when Anna sang "Wind Beneath My Wings."

Anna was inconsolable. She sobbed as she viewed the white flowers adorning the casket and the white stuffed bear draped with a rosary sitting beneath the casket. Although she tried to read a Bible passage to the congregation, she only managed to say "The swords of the just are in the hands of God..." She fell apart after that.

Surprisingly, Diana Marshall, Anna's attorney, was the one to stand and eulogize. According to *People* magazine, Marshall said, "I am here today to talk about love. I have never known a relationship that embodied love as much as this one. Anna, if Howard were here today, he would say to you, 'Don't cry, Precious Package, my Lady Love.' And in years to come, when you see yourself succeeding, as you will, because you are strong, you will say to yourself, 'Hello, Howard. I'm succeeding. I've got my chin up.'"

Ray Martino, who was so new to Anna's life that he'd only met Howard a few times, said that those brief moments with Anna and Howard "taught him the meaning of love."

Although most of the media were held outside the sanctuary, Smith did allow the Houston bureau chief for *People* magazine to sit among the mourners, as well as cameras from *Extra*, a daily entertainment television program.

J. Howard Marshall's death was treated like sideshow entertainment. The news stories all included pictures of Anna Nicole looking her most lascivious.

David Letterman quipped that his ovation lasted longer than an Anna Nicole Smith mourning period.

Not to be outdone, Jay Leno included her in his monologue. "She said she's getting tired of defending her feelings toward her late husband—she says she worshiped the ground he struck oil on."

But why shouldn't they have their fun? It's not as if the wedding and the funeral weren't all played out in every tabloid and magazine.

Extra filmed the candelabra, her white gown, the piano player. When Anna broke down, whispering "I'm sorry, I can't right now," it was said to a reporter and caught on film.

Oddly, caterers from Magnolia Grill stood by outside with the rest of the journalists. They served hors d'oeuvres of goose liver and salmon pate and Perrier. A harpist strummed as mourners, all from Anna's side of the family, filed out at the end of the service.

Anna didn't stop to eat. A black limousine waited for her at the entrance. She left with Daniel and new best friend Ray Martino.

Maxine Mesinger, the gossip columnist for the *Houston Chronicle* wrote, in her August 11 column, that "If anyone has any idea of trying to 'crash' the memorial service Sunday, August 13, for oilman J. Howard Marshall II, forget it. His son is in charge of Sunday's service and said, 'All I want is to honor my dad here in Houston, where he lived most of his life.' The family expects friends and business associates to fly in from both coasts for the memorial; Marshall had many friends in high places. There will be heavy security at Geo. H. Lewis & Sons on Sunday, both before and after the service. The funeral home's head honcho, Bob Jones, will be given the list of invited guests, and only persons on that list will be admitted. Pierce Marshall pointed out that his father came from a small Quaker family in a suburb of Philadelphia. Litany is limited in a Quaker funeral, and Pierce will stick with its customs for the memorial."

Mesinger quotes Jones saying, "I handled the Howard Hughes funeral, and this one's worse."

Of course, at the time of both funerals, the decision had not been reached as to what to actually do with Marshall's body.

Under Texas law, the widow is supposed to have first say on such matters as disposition of the body, but Pierce Marshall contended that his power of attorney entitled him to arrange for the funeral, and dispose of the body.

In a bizarre aside, *People* magazine quotes a Geo. H. Lewis & Sons staffer as saying "[Anna Nicole] wanted to take the coffin out to her ranch and set him up on the patio deck. I had to talk her out of it—I could just see him sliding into the swimming pool."

Chapter 33

On Monday, August 14, 1995, Anna had her day in court. Although she'd already had a funeral for her husband, the body had yet to be interred.

Pierce insisted that he had signed a funeral contract in January designating him to make arrangements, including the cremation of his father's remains.

Anna's lawyer Suzie Kornblit was quoted in *USA Today*. "Our position is that it's extremely inappropriate for the son...to make this contract without consultation with the wife. If it were Howard's wish to be cremated, Anna would have honored his wish."

Kornblit's contention was that Pierce made the contract when "his dad was sick in the hospital and Anna was at his bedside."

In preparation for the upcoming, bigger legal battle over Marshall's estate, Kornbilt made it clear that "Howard slept the night at their ranch many times. He's also slept the night at her L.A. house...She has slept the night with him in his Texas house."

The disagreement about Marshall's body ended with an out-of-court settlement. Probate Judge Jim Scanlon decreed that Pierce and Anna would equally divide Marshall's ashes after he was cremated.

Anna had opposed the cremation on religious grounds. It seems she had recently converted to Catholicism.

According to her cousin, Melinda, it was the influence of movie director Ray Martino that had Anna questioning her beliefs. After working with him on one of her movies, Ray supposedly persuaded Anna that her immortal soul was in danger and that converting to Catholicism was the answer. Melinda also reported that Ray is still trying to "cast the demons" out from Anna, using candles, prayers, and other rituals. A priest was not present during these ceremonies.

However, Anna did speak with Father Bruce Noble after Marshall's death. He assured her that cremation was accepted by the Catholic Church. That conversation took place prior to the hearing, so Anna was willing to concede the issue to Pierce.

She didn't fare so well at the actual hearing, however. According to the *Houston Chronicle*, Anna, had to be led from the courtroom due to an attack of nausea.

The attorneys from both sides went behind locked doors to negotiate and finally reached agreement late in the afternoon.

Pierce and his attorneys did not comment, but Anna told the *Chronicle*, "I think it's fair. I'm glad it's over. Thank you for coming."

After that, Diana Marshall read the following statement to the press:

"E. Pierce Marshall and Anna Nicole Smith have reached an agreement today whereby J. Howard Marshall's remains will be cremated, and the remains will be divided and disposed of by agreement of the parties. Each of the parties believes that this agreement best serves the interests of J. Howard Marshall II with respect."

According to those in attendance, Anna's main argument with regard to the entire proceeding was that she wanted acknowledgment from Pierce that as Howard's widow, she was entitled to some respect.

This court session dealt only with one issue—the disposition of Marshall's body. Nothing was settled about his estate.

Interestingly, Maxine Mesinger, in her August 16 column, stated that insiders told her that although Howard Marshall "lived very comfortably...his wealth was enormously exaggerated— including *Forbes'* multimillion-dollar estimate in the early 1980s."

Chapter 34

On August 18, a Los Angeles court found that Anna Nicole Smith Marshall had failed to follow through on her lawsuit against Maria Antonia Cerrato and therefore had to pay out damages. Anna's attorney declared that no guilt was admitted and that she would immediately file an appeal.

According to Kelly Moore, another of Smith's attorneys, Anna's countersuit was effectively dismissed because she failed to comply with an evidence procedure.

Moore told the Associated Press that "There is no admission of guilt in this."

At the same time, ex-bodyguard Pierre DeJean was busy talking to the press.

He told the *National Examiner* that "I can put the brakes on that inheritance so fast, it will make her head spin."

DeJean reiterated his claims that he had an affair with Anna after her marriage to Marshall. He also said he had an explicit videotape to prove it, but as of this writing, the tape has never surfaced.

He also told the *Examiner* that, "Pierce and Anna Nicole cannot stand each other. Even before Marshall's death, Pierce's people came to me. I substantiated my relationship with Anna."

Of course, this comes from a man who has lied, on several occasions, to us. He had once embellished on his bodyguard-to-the-stars story, saying when he worked for Aresenio Hall, he, Hall, and Eddie Murphy had been together in the Polo Lounge on a certain night. Eric found out that DeJean hadn't been there at all, and neither had Mr. Hall or Mr. Murphy.

Anna Nicole responded to *National Examiner* reporters that "pictures taken of them kissing and cuddling prove absolutely nothing. 'If I like someone, I'm very touch-feely. He's just out to cash in.'"

On August 19, the *Globe* printed yet another damaging report about Anna Nicole. Daniel Ross, the guy she'd been seeing a year before her marriage to Marshall, claimed that Anna "had a whole wardrobe full of sexy lingerie, see-through stuff. She also had leather ties and gags. And canes, you know, for sadomasochistic sessions."

Ross said that she asked him to try on some costumes, including a pair of leather trunks.

In the terribly unflattering piece, Ross is quoted about how much Anna likes to eat. The whole article was ugly—and completely irrelevant to anything going on at the time. The *Globe* clearly had nothing relevant to say, so it dug for dirt in order to run something.

Another item that made the papers was the emergency surgery that took place on November 28, 1994. One of Anna's breast implants had ruptured and was leaking inside her body. Anna had opted for saline implants, and one was defective.

Anna herself told *Globe* reporters that "My left breast was shrunken and withered. It was half the size of my right one. I called my doc and screamed—This is my life, my whole world. I can't look like this!"

The surgery took three hours, and according to Anna, "They had to fight to wake me from the anesthetic. I nearly lost my breasts—and my life."

One of the hospital staff commented that "Anna was a total pain in the ass. A big crybaby." She ordered people around, demanded drugs, and when she couldn't get them, she went off on the nurses.

Two interesting things came out of that hospital stay. One was that Anna ended up with larger breasts, and the other was her bodyguard Pierre DeJean was out, and Clay Spires was back in.

Chapter 35

*D*espite the turmoil in her life, Anna Nicole continued to work, claiming she had no money at all, and to fight with Pierce to get her share of Howard's fortune.

So it was up to Diana Marshall, Anna's attorney, to focus on getting Anna her portion of J. Howard Marshall's estate. It didn't matter that Anna Nicole wasn't mentioned in Marshall's 1992 will. State law clearly entitled Smith to half of whatever her late husband earned during their fourteen-month marriage.

What did bother her, Diana stated, was "the blizzard of documents that were put in front of Howard Marshall to sign two weeks after his marriage. He signed all of them in an almost completely illegible fashion, which makes sense because he couldn't read at the time, according to his doctors."

Included in the "blizzard" was the power of attorney, giving Pierce the legal right to control the J. Howard Marshall II Living

Trust, which is the full beneficiary of the will filed August 8 in Louisiana.

Diana Marshal claimed that the power of attorney was "basically an attempt to remove Howard Marshall from control of his estate."

Diana Marshall made it clear that Anna wished to resolve the matter of the estate out of court.

Of course, what that estate consisted of was unknown by Smith or her attorneys. Many figures had been batted about—everything from $3 billion to only a few million. Diana Marshall indicated that the true amount would be revealed at some point.

Anna was busy doing some maneuvering on her own. She had granted an interview to *People* magazine and allowed their photographer to take pictures during the funeral service. The picture that appeared in the August 21 issue, shows Anna, dressed in her white gown, holding her tiny black dog, Beauty. However, Anna's breast had come out of the bra cup, and her nipple is clearly visible in the photograph. Behind her, Ray Martino, the man Anna's cousin, called "Svengali" was at her side. By this time, Martino had become Anna's confidant.

Anna had systematically alienated her family. First, Kay Beall, the woman Anna claimed raised her, was cut off. Then her Aunt and Uncle Tabers were sent packing. Even her mother, Virgie, was on shaky ground.

But it was Diana Marshall's strategy to bring repeated declarations of the love shared by young Anna and her husband directly to the public.

Pierce had stopped Anna's $50,000-a-month allowance, and, according to *People*, had accused her of defrauding his father "by way of excessive gifts or transfers of community property to strangers of the marriage, with some of whom she has had adulterous affairs."

In response, Smith quoted a letter from her husband that read, in part, "I don't object to his being guardian for my affairs, matter of fact he runs a lot of businesses and does very good. But he has no business coming between my wife and myself."

Pierce didn't take any of this lying down. Maxine Mesinger, in her Big City Beat column in the *Houston Chronicle* reported that Pierce Marshall filed suit against attorney Diana Marshall, the firm of Schechter & Marshall, and attorney Suzie Kornblit. The charge? Defamation of character.

According to court papers filed in Dallas, Pierce sued Diana Marshall for the statement that she was "bothered" by the fact that two weeks after the marriage between Marshall and Anna Nicole, Marshall signed a "blizzard" of documents at a time when his doctors said he couldn't read, and that his signature was a "almost completely illegible...a squiggle."

Pierce called the accusations a "smear campaign" designed to help Anna Nicole get a large financial settlement from his father's estate.

According to the *Houston Chronicle*, Pierce Marshall claimed these slurs had cause him "emotional distress, embarrassment and humiliation," and that Pierce was entitled to unspecified damages for harm to his reputation.

The suit read in part, "Diana Marshall intended the listener and/or reader of her statements to understand that her statements meant E. Pierce Marshall used fraud and/or forgery wrongfully to steal control of the J. Howard Marshall II Living Trust from his own father."

Kornblit, he claimed, made "defamatory personal attacks" during a separate news interview. Allegedly, Kornblit characterized Pierce as "greedy and miserly...a real control freak."

Diana Marshall called the suit "frivolous litigation." She then proceeded to countersue him to recover more than $16,000 she fronted for J. Howard Marshall's funeral at the Geo. H. Lewis Funeral Home. The costs were for both the services held by Anna Nicole and E. Pierce Marshall.

In January 1996, J. Howard's other son jumped into the fray. J. Howard Marshall III opposed the probate of his father's will. He accused his brother, Pierce, of taking advantage of their father's weakened condition and poor eyesight to get the older Marshall to sign the power of attorney.

The petition filed on behalf of J. Howard III maintained that Pierce "embarked on a concerted course of conduct to gain complete control of assets" when J. Howard II "could not see what he was signing."

In effect the older brother was coming out on Anna Nicole's side. His lawyer, Jack W. Lawter, Jr., said the equitable solution would be for the estate to be divided into three equal parts going to Pierce, J. Howard III—and the widow, Anna Nicole Smith. Such an outcome would keep Anna in bonbons for a long time.

So, life continued for Anna, and with a new television season came a guest role on ABC's *The Naked Truth*. Anna played herself—a media darling tailed relentlessly by tabloid journalists. No acting was required, although the part did require her to have a sense of humor about herself. In the show, Nora Wilde, played by Tea Leoni, goes after pictures of Anna at the gynecologist's office. Classy? No. Amusing? Barely. But it served its purpose.

Anna was on the screen, viewers were reminded yet again that she was, in every way, bigger than life, and she got paid. Marshall had been in the hospital when the episode was shot, and it aired just after he died.

The *Houston Chronicle* said that "The raunchy pilot is being cleaned up, but only because the worst jokes were at the expense of the pilot's guest star, Anna Nicole Smith. Since it taped, Smith's husband died here in Houston, and in deference to her trials and mourning, they're cleaning up her part of the act."

It's hard to imagine what the original was like, if that was the cleaned-up version. How many tasteful shows center around a urine specimen?

To add to Anna's already overflowing "cup," the Superior Court of the State of California ruled in favor of Maria Cerrato and ordered Anna to pay $110,000 in special damages, $416,952 in general damages, and $250,000 in punitive damages. In addition, Anna was to pay Maria's attorneys' fees to the tune of $75,000 and $4,044.54 worth of disbursements, plus interest.

*A*nna starred in *To the Limit*, a sexploitation film directed by Ray Martino. Although she'd told a reporter that "People suppose that because I've done *Playboy*, I'm open for nudity all the time. But that's not correct. If I was in a movie like *Basic Instinct* and had to do a nude scene, I would. But I'm not going to take my clothes off for some bit part."

Her role in *To the Limit* wasn't a bit part, but it's no *Basic Instinct*, either. Anna is nude a great deal of the time. She masturbates in a bathtub, then again in a shower. Revealing herself wasn't enough to make the movie a hit—it went straight to video.

Variety gave a surprisingly positive review of *To the Limit*. Despite calling it a "trash actioner," they said that the movie was no worse than hundreds of others. For *Variety*, that wasn't half bad.

"When not required to speak, however, the Texan mega-baby makes a formidable presence, especially for one brief moment in reel three when she suddenly changes from a brain-dead bimbo to a rod-wielding hard-ass."

While they did say that Raymond Martino's direction is large-ly pedestrian, they pointed out that Smith's soft-core interludes feature occasional full-frontals and that the film should see "robust trade across vid counters."

A friend said: "Anna really hoped this movie would catapult her career. But it nosedived."

In an interview with the German tabloid *Neue Revue*, Anna, there to promote *To the Limit*, was asked about the shower head scene. "Oooh," she moaned. "Closed eyes all the way. It was very intimate."

On why she wanted the film to do well: "It's not because of the money. I don't like to talk about money."

When asked her fondest wish, Anna told the reporter that she'd like to have another baby, a little girl. "I pray with my rosary every evening," she said. "Honestly, I beg God to protect me and my son, and that he will give me another great love with whom I could fly away—like Peter Pan in the storybook."

Chapter 36

On November 6, 1995, paramedics were called once again to rescue Anna Nicole. It was reported in the *Star* that she was at her boyfriend, Ray Martino's home, and it was he who called 911. According to the *Houston Chronicle*, the incident took place at Anna Nicole's Brentwood home, where her housekeeper called for help.

In either case, paramedics found Anna limp on the floor. They were told she'd had several seizures prior to their arrival. They took her to St. Joseph's Medical Center in Burbank, where she was immediately listed in critical condition.

Diana Marshall insisted that Anna had again had a reaction to pain medication prescribed for migraine headaches. The same story had been told the last time Anna had been rushed to the hospital after she'd combined quantities of alcohol, painkillers, and tranquilizers.

"Anna was packing at home to go to London for a modeling assignment," Diana Marshall told reporters. "She even had her plane ticket in her bag. People see her as invincible and healthy, but she gets these very bad problems with headaches. It is not a drug overdose."

Nassir Samirami told *Star* reporters, "Anna had a seizure. She's going to be okay."

Tony Angeloti, a spokesman for the model, said, "Anna gets migraines a couple of times a month and takes medication for them. She's been through a lot of trauma, at it takes some time for her to come back."

The news blanketed the media. Not just tabloids, but news shows including CNN reported that Anna had been rushed to the hospital. Although the reporters dutifully quoted the "migraine" story, every one of them implied that Anna had overdosed.

*A*nna was released on Sunday, November 12, but she didn't go home. First reports indicated she was recuperating at an "undisclosed location." It was soon discovered, however, that Anna Nicole went straight to the Betty Ford clinic, the drug rehab center so popular with movie stars and rock idols.

Friends were immediately interviewed, and the *Globe* even managed to get a quote from reclusive Billy Wayne Smith, Anna's first husband. Smith, Daniel's father, said, "She seems to have a serious drug problem, and I'm worried about Daniel. I want to find out if I might be awarded sole custody of our boy."

Another unnamed source said in the same article, "Everyone knows Anna's fond of certain pills."

Hard Copy was the first to break the news that Anna had gone to Betty Ford. They ran pictures of Anna Nicole in a wheelchair, on the grounds of the expensive clinic. Shortly after that, the *Globe* ran the same pictures in an article festooned with the headlines: "Texas tycoon's pinup playmate fights for her life in Betty Ford. Drug nightmare puts Anna Nicole in a wheelchair."

Despite the garish headline, the news in the article was devastating: Anna Nicole had suffered possible brain damage.

"Doctors are worried her heart may have stopped, causing permanent brain damage," one "insider" said. "There seems to be some sort of impairment—doctors hope it's temporary."

It's clear something had gone seriously wrong. One of the rules at the clinic is that no matter what, patients must walk to and from the cafeteria for meals. But Anna Nicole has been taken in her wheelchair. "Another rule there is patients are required to walk and talk with other patients. It's considered an important part of the therapy. Anna Nicole is not fraternizing with the other patients."

Another source reported that "Anna acts very depressed and seems ashamed of the way she looks. She hides her face in the cafeteria. Right after she arrived, she wouldn't or couldn't get out of bed until they brought in a woman to do her hair."

And still, Diana Marshall insisted Anna had a bad reaction from migraine medication.

"That's baloney," one friend said. "She was admitted as an OD. Doctors are afraid there's permanent brain damage. They haven't established that yet. She's scheduled to have a lot of tests done."

According to Melinda Beall, Anna checked herself out of rehab after a few days. Virgie talked to Melinda, telling her that Anna was fine, no brain damage. Melinda thought it was surprising that the issue of permanent injury had come up, but she added the obvious, Anna liked taking drugs.

Chapter 37

*I*n the January 1995 issue of *Glamour* magazine, BKG Youth Inc., a New York City research firm, asked one thousand men if they would be more likely to fantasize about superwaif Kate Moss or former Guess? model Anna Nicole Smith. Sixty-nine percent said Anna Nicole.

In *SPY* magazine's 1994 Annual Census of the Top 100 Most Annoying, Alarming, and Appalling People, Places and Things, Anna Nicole came in fifty-fourth, just after Counting Crows and in front of Courtney Love.

On *Entertainment Tonight*, the host claimed that Anna's fifteen minutes of fame were up.

On the other hand, Anna is now the spokesmodel for LIVE, a unisex perfume from Wilshire Fragrance. The ad campaign invites consumers to "Get Live With Anna."

Wilshire president Peter Klamka told *W* magazine that "Guess? proved she can sell to women, and *Playboy* proved she can sell to men." He was very excited about the campaign and hoped the relationship with Anna lasted a very long time.

For a few months, Anna was also the new spokesmodel for Lane Bryant, the clothing store for women sized 14 through 26. The ad campaign pictured Anna in different, beautiful poses, and the caption read "What Real Women Wear." However, according to *Daily Variety*, Lane Bryant dissolved that relationship shortly after she left the rehabilitation center. The article went on to say that "A spokesman for Smith said she was only engaged for a couple of appearances with Lane Bryant and denied she was replaced."

To add to her woes, ex-husband Billy Wayne Smith resurfaced on the pages of the December 26, 1995, *Globe*.

He tells the familiar tale of how they'd met and wed, but in his version, Anna was the aggressor. She approached him for the marriage, was the aggressor in bed. He also claimed that their breakup had nothing to do with his violence toward her. On the contrary, he said that the breakup was due to a one-night spat about sex— he wanted it, she didn't. "I was stunned," he says. "She never turned me down for sex before." The next day she walked out on him.

The family disputed this version and went on to say that despite Smith's claim that "the only thing in the world I really want [is] to see Daniel again," he never lifted a finger to find the boy, let alone check on his welfare.

Regardless of the veracity of Billy Smith's assertions, it's very clear Anna Nicole is a troubled young woman. Her family remains concerned. Not just about the alienation, or about the drugs, but about her relationship with Raymond Martino. In Kay's opinion,

Raymond is encouraging Anna to keep away from her family and friends as he wishes her to be totally dependent upon him.

Melinda is worried, too. "Anna's really a nice person," she said. "The money gets in the way sometimes. She's really caring. She's bought me school clothes. She always promised momma a car when she got rich. And she did that."

She recalled an earlier day, a more innocent time, when she traveled everywhere with Anna and Daniel. When they were still close.

Anna liked nothing better than to have Melinda play "doctor" on her back. Anna would lie, face down, in her bed, without her top, and Melinda would find objects—forks, spoons, brushes, whatever, and rub Anna's back with them—Anna would have to guess what the objects were.

That hasn't happened in a long, long time.

What has happened is that Anna checked herself into the hospital for depression twice. Once in May, 1995 and once in July 1995.

Chapter 38

*O*nce again, we watched the *Howard Stern Show* on television. Stern introduced Anna Nicole off camera, while the viewers saw her in the green room, accompanied by Daniel and the omnipresent Raymond Martino.

Dressed in jeans and a white-cropped long-sleeved blouse, a dangling white crucifix and, of course, the 22-carat ring, Anna picked up a clipboard and walked to the studio.

It was hard to reconcile the woman who sat down, her burgundy lipstick so garish it eclipsed, for the moment, her cleavage, with the woman who'd shyly called Larry King "sir" only a few years before.

This woman looked hard, tough, slutty. Instead of the luminous beauty ready to take on the world, she appeared broken by the fame she'd wanted so badly.

From the first word out of her mouth, it was painfully clear she was completely wrecked on drugs. The words slurred together, her eyes barely opened, and when they did, there was no life in them at all. She asked Howard to repeat his questions and then struggled to find simple answers.

Of course, Stern pounced, ready with his patented sexual banter to please his fans.

"Look at the chest on you," he said. "Let me soak you in. Give her a banana. Let's see what she does."

Anna didn't even hesitate—she wrapped her lips around the fruit with a practiced pout.

The conversation was nonsense. There was nothing said that didn't have a sexual intent. But then, that's Howard Stern.

Anna talked baby-talk, smiled often, gave inappropriate answers.

She didn't call Stern "sir." She didn't blush.

It was heartbreaking.

Where was Vickie Lynn Hogan? Had fame taken all the joy from her life? Why had things gone so wrong?

Perhaps the answer lies with the kind of fame Anna went after so voraciously. Her dream was to be a celebrity. In that, she's been remarkably successful. She's known from Alaska to Zaire, as popular in Germany as in Texas. But what is she known for?

A body that owes more to the surgeon's knife than mother nature. She's come to personify the illicit dreams of adolescent boys of all ages. The love affair with the camera has created an unwholesome image, a tragedy, not a triumph. She's become a slave to her own desires, a victim of the tabloid press that made her a household name.

The price she's paid has been enormous. But she had no arsenal to fend off the negative aspects of fame. No knowledge of the ways of the world. The girl had one asset—a face of extraordinary beauty. Of course, she had breast augmentation surgeries. Because that increased her value in a world that honors *Playboy* Playmates with the same fervor as football heros.

Playboy, incidentally, is not ready to give up on Anna Nicole, despite her grotesque weight gain. In the spring of 1996, it was reported the magazine is paying her $500,000 for another photo shoot. *Playboy* is also supposed to be picking up the tab for her weight-reduction program–gym, trainer, chef, the works.

That matters little to her Aunt Kay who told D'eva just the other night that all she wanted was to have Vickie back. To once again see the sweet girl from Mexia who liked garage sales and Jim's Krispy Fried Chicken. There's still time. After all...Anna Nicole Smith is only twenty-eight years old.

Afterword

Some additional thoughts from two who loved her as Vickie Lynn Hogan, and if truth be told, still love her as Anna Nicole Smith.

Anna and Melinda Beall had a very close relationship. They were more than cousins; they even referred to themselves as sisters. Melinda spent a great deal of time with Anna up until July 1995.

"I used to stay around Anna all the time," she told us during a long lunch in Mexia. "I realize that now. My mom [Kay Beall] used to say that I loved Anna more than her. Ever since I was a little girl, I've been around her a lot. She was like a sister to me. I used to watch Daniel a lot. I loved him to death. Now that we're apart, I always miss them."

Melinda was seventeen when we spoke with her. She was living in a small trailer, with her mother Kay and Kay's new husband. It's clear that life hasn't been easy for them. The furniture is old,

201

the carpet worn. There is very little that is beautiful. Except for one picture. A large portrait of Anna Nicole, back when she was still Vickie Lynn Smith. In the portrait, she holds baby Daniel. There is something innocent and sweet and shy about it. It's no wonder that portrait, out of the hundreds that have been taken since, hangs in Melinda's bedroom.

"The only thing that I know of that would make Anna happy was me and Daniel. The only thing that ever made her happy. She was happy around Mom. Mom got tired of running around with her. Floyd was hired as her secretary. But there were odd hours. She would call at two or three in the morning, saying 'I need this and that' and she always wanted him to go get her donuts. Where in the heck do you find donuts at three in the morning?"

"Was she happy here in Mexia at all?" Eric asked.

"I don't think so. She's always wanted to be a movie star and a model and everything. When she got her break in *Playboy*, I think she was really happy."

"Does Daniel still sleep with her?"

"Yes," Melinda said, shaking her head. "Daniel's a mamma's boy. I was told about an incident...where she took a gun to her head in front of Daniel and she told him that she was going to blow her brains out. I don't think that's good for Daniel."

"You saw that?"

"No, I believe it was Uncle Minnow [Melvin Tabers] that told me about it. Nassir Samirami, better known as Sam, her driver, he told Uncle Minnow that he saw her take a gun to her head and threaten to blow her brains out. I really don't think that's healthy for a little boy."

"Was this out at the ranch?"

"No, it was in Los Angeles. In Brentwood."

"Were you out there when she had her overdose in 1994?" D'eva asked. "When Pierre called 911?"

"No. She didn't overdose. You want me to tell you what she did? She drank and took her pills together. It made her pass out. I think it was Pierre who freaked out and called an ambulance. She was just like normal to me. It's Pierre that freaked out and called 911. You remember that one incident in Los Angeles when they had all that coverage? When she was with Daniel Ross?"

"You met him?"

"Yes, I did. He was okay. He seemed nice to me, but Anna didn't like him that much. It was the same deal with Daniel Ross. She just took too much alcohol with her pills."

Melinda got up then and brought some pictures for us to see. They were photos from Christmas, with Anna, Daniel, and Melinda sitting by a beautifully decorated tree at the ranch house.

"Tell me about Christmas," D'eva said.

"Christmas was okay. I think everybody got a little greedy the last Christmas we all went to. The one when Mom got her car and Maria got her car at the same time. Anna bought Virgie a big screen TV. I thought it was really greedy. Right after Virgie got the TV, she left. It wasn't no fun. We had sandwiches and Kool-aid. It was just a greedy Christmas. There was no love in it. Everybody got their presents and left."

"Did Anna get upset?"

"Yes. The day after, we had Christmas with Howard. That was a real Christmas. I liked it. Vickie fooled him. She told him she cooked the dinner and she didn't because I went to Brookshire grocery store to get something. She took it out of the platters and put it in bowls and stuff. She told him it was all homemade!"

"But you don't see a lot of her now, do you?"

"No. She talks to Virgie."

"So she's pretty much alone?"

"Yes, she talks to Aunt Virgie sometimes. Anna brought that on for herself. If she would have been a little bit nicer to everybody, maybe she could have... She started snapping at everybody. Every time something came up missing around the house, she said I stole it. I would never steal anything from her. I love her."

"Does she know you love her?"

"I guess. She used to say it to me. She thinks that my mom did something wrong, too. My mom didn't do nothing to her. I take that back. My mom cursed her out before she walked out the door. That's only because they couldn't put up with her anymore."

"What do you think is changing her?"

"I think the money is changing her. If she didn't have the money, she'd probably be the same old Vickie that she used to be. I like the old Vickie better than I like Anna Nicole. Vickie used to do my nails. We were a really tight family. We used to be really close. I think my grandmother kept us together. When my grandmother died, the family just pulled apart. We're not really that tight anymore."

"Was Anna pretty close to your grandmother?"

"Granny was the sweetest lady. Vickie used to call her Country Granny. Vickie would come every Thanksgiving and Christmas and visited us after she went to Houston. [Since Granny died] we really don't have Christmas anymore. We have them, but it's no big deal. Because granny's not here. I lived with her most of my life. My mom would try to take me home, and granny would cry and say that dad would beat me. She wanted me there. I basically lived with my grandmother until I was thirteen. Then I moved up with Anna."

"How often do you talk to Anna now?"

"Oh, I talk to her regularly. She said that she was going to pay my driver's education money, but I don't know. I talked to Aunt Virgie just last week. She's working three jobs plus her police job to pay her bills. Aunt Virgie does a police watch on the horses on the weekends. She works at Bennigan's. She works at Kroger's as a guard. She has to do all that to pay her bills."

"So do you call Anna? Or does she call you?"

"She calls me. She's got blocks on all her phone numbers so that nobody can call her collect.... Do you know how much money she earns? She gets over $40,000 or $50,000 a month. Pierce was giving her over $30,000 a month. She used to get over $100,000. Now, $30,000 barely pays her bills. That's probably why she's so anxious about this whole thing with Pierce...."

"Does he still pay her?"

"He don't have to. A while ago, she told me that she would kill to go to a garage sale again. She can't do that. We used to go to a lot of garage sales. It's no big deal down here. It's a fun thing to do. Now Anna can't have that image. She said that she would kill to just go and mess up for fun. She said that everywhere she goes, publicity gets her and tabloids are out to get her. So she doesn't do anything for fun anymore."

*A*nna Nicole is also estranged from her Uncle Melvin, who the family calls Uncle Minnow. Although he worked for Anna at the ranch, things fell apart when he became ill. He could no longer take care of the livestock or the grounds once his heart went bad. But the real bone of contention was that Anna believes Melvin stole from her, despite the fact that he was forced to sell some of the cattle in order to pay for the horse feed. According to

Kay and Melinda, Anna hadn't paid Melvin in five or six months nor did she give him any money to maintain the grounds and the animals. Finally, Melvin and his wife sold the horses and moved back to Livingston, Texas. They haven't spoken to Anna Nicole since.

*A*nna Nicole had been so close to her Aunt Kay, that she called her "mama," and quite a few people thought they were mother and daughter. In addition to practically raising her as a child, Kay spent a great deal of time travelling; with Anna on photo shoots and taking care of Daniel.

However, they, too, had an estrangement that left them on nonspeaking terms. Kay's theory on this is that Anna has difficulty with people who truly care about her. She remembers Al Bolt and Alan Mielsch, how they both loved Anna. She cut them loose. She's always run from those closest to her, manufacturing problems if none existed.

"When she was little, she lived with Virgie, but she would come over any chance she got to stay with me. I was young and funny and she could talk to me. She would come over and spend the weekends or school vacations. She would stay as much as her mom would let her. But then she would have these boyfriends during high school. She would run away from those relationships. If they showed any kind of real feelings for her, she would run away."

A year after Anna worked for Guess?, she asked Kay and Melinda to prove their love in an unconventional way. She took them to a small tatoo parlor in Humble, Texas, called Bubba's Skin Pen. She asked them each to get a tatoo—of her face. Kay had one put on her back. Melinda's went on her ankle.

About six months after that, Anna and Kay fell out. Kay got

aggravated when Anna accused Melinda and ex-boyfriend Floyd of stealing. Anna would get drunk and yell at Kay. It was too stressful. Kay told Anna that she wanted to go home because she was sick and tired and couldn't take it anymore.

Kay didn't expect the estrangement to last long, but it did.

"I told Virgie to tell her that I was getting married," Kay said. "She didn't say that she wanted to come down here and visit or nothing. She's never met my new husband. He's a wonderful man. You put in that book that Mama Two loves her with all her heart. That's what she always called me. Mama Two. She's a good girl. If people would just love her for who she is and not for what they think she should be. I love her. I will always love her. I wouldn't care if she would stab me in the back. She's still one of my kids."